A Pioneer Son at Sea

UNIVERSITY PRESS OF FLORIDA

Florida A&M University, Tallahassee
Florida Atlantic University, Boca Raton
Florida Gulf Coast University, Ft. Myers
Florida International University, Miami
Florida State University, Tallahassee
New College of Florida, Sarasota
University of Central Florida, Orlando
University of Florida, Gainesville
University of North Florida, Jacksonville
University of South Florida, Tampa
University of West Florida, Pensacola

A Pioneer Son at Sea

Fishing Tales of Old Florida

~~~~~~

Gilbert L. Voss

Edited by Robert S. Voss

UNIVERSITY PRESS OF FLORIDA

Gainesville / Tallahassee / Tampa / Boca Raton

Pensacola / Orlando / Miami / Jacksonville / Ft. Myers / Sarasota

Frontispiece: Gilbert L. Voss. Photographer unknown, ca. 1937

This book may be available in an electronic edition.

21 20 19 18 17 16   6 5 4 3 2 1

Library of Congress Control Number: 2015952080
ISBN 978-0-8130-6252-5

The University Press of Florida is the scholarly publishing agency for the State University System of Florida, comprising Florida A&M University, Florida Atlantic University, Florida Gulf Coast University, Florida International University, Florida State University, New College of Florida, University of Central Florida, University of Florida, University of North Florida, University of South Florida, and University of West Florida.

University Press of Florida
15 Northwest 15th Street
Gainesville, FL 32611-2079
http://www.upf.com

For Nicholas and Matthew,
both enthusiastic fishermen,
who would have enjoyed
knowing their grandfather.

"There is no more intimate relationship we can have with our environment than to eat from it."

Paul Greenberg, *American Catch: The Fight for Our Local Seafood*

"Nothing will destroy the science and mission of conservation biology faster than a generation or two of biologists raised on dead facts and technology and lacking direct, personal experience with Nature."

Reed F. Noss, "The Naturalists Are Dying Off"

Contents

Foreword

My father, Gilbert L. Voss ("Gil" to family and friends), was a marine biologist and conservationist who worked and taught for many years at the Marine Laboratory of the University of Miami on Virginia Key. An internationally recognized specialist on cephalopods—octopus, cuttlefish, and squid—he also directed the University of Miami's ambitious deep-sea trawling program in the 1960s, served as chief scientist on numerous oceanographic cruises, edited the *Bulletin of Marine Science*, and established the laboratory's renowned marine invertebrate museum. Alarmed by the deteriorating condition of south Florida's coral reefs, he was active in local conservation movements, and he was one of the chief proponents of the John Pennekamp Coral Reef State Park, the first undersea park in the United States. Over the course of his professional career he published well over a hundred scientific reports as well as several popular books on oceanography, seashore life, and coral reefs. Many of the doctoral students he mentored went on to become influential marine biologists at universities, museums, and laboratories across the country and abroad.

Key to Gil's effectiveness in many aspects of his professional career were deep family roots in Florida history; a lifelong familiarity with both the seashore and the open ocean; an intimate knowledge of ships, engines, nets, and other marine hardware; and an enduring affection for fishermen and their ways. Few who knew him only as a researcher, fellow committee member, or classroom lecturer—usually dressed, like most scientists of his generation, in a coat and tie—were fully aware of his non-academic background, nor did they know that science was a late calling. Born to pioneer parents on Lake Worth, Gil grew to manhood during the Depression, fishing the rich waters of the state, which then teemed with marine life. After four years in the U.S. Coast Guard during World War II, he fished again for a while with his brothers before deciding to go back to school on the G.I. Bill. Gil had always wanted to write and intended to become a professional author, but the fisherman-writer was captivated by an introductory zoology course at the University of Miami and began a long career in biological oceanography instead.

Late in life Gil completed a memoir of his early experiences fishing in Florida. Set in the 1930s and 1940s, these stories vividly re-create his years as a fisherman and as a coastguardsman working among fishermen on both coasts of the peninsula. His accounts depict vanished scenes almost unimaginable to modern residents of the state. Long before the plague of hotels, condominiums, and strip malls that now disfigure so much of our coastline, Florida was home to dozens of commercial fisheries and to ethnically diverse communities of rugged individuals who made their living from the sea. Few now remember this rich fabric of indigenous Florida lifeways, which were once a vital part of the state's economy.

At various times in his early days Gil netted for mackerel, handlined for kingfish, tied up alongside the rowdy-crewed snapper fleet at Carrabelle, mated for his brothers in the early days of charterboat fishing, made friends among the sponge divers at Tarpon Springs, placated angry oystermen at Crystal River, and fished for mullet from airboats at Flamingo. Outsized personalities inhabit these stories: crackers, Greek spongers, Cuban *vivero* captains, conchs, and a host of minor but unforgettable characters. These were men who once went down to the sea in ships, and the sea supported them.

These stories make good reading, but they are also remarkable as formative chapters in the life of a scientist who later made a difference, working tirelessly to preserve south Florida's endangered marine habitats. Is there a connection? Many prominent naturalists and conservationists of the twentieth century grew up fishing, hunting, trapping, or collecting. Although such activities may seem exploitative to armchair environmentalists, subsistence-level involvement with nature yields deep knowledge of how organisms live and ecosystems function. Can such fertile life experiences be sustained in an increasingly virtual world? Can anyone better defend the oceans than those who once wrested a living from the waves?

Gil's maternal grandfather, Hannibal Dillingham Pierce, was something of an adventurer, and it is a minor miracle that he survived to raise a family on the southeast coast of Florida. Born in Maine in 1834, Hannibal ran away to sea at sixteen and, among other escapades, went whaling in the Arctic Ocean, prospected for gold in Australia, and was shipwrecked at least twice, the last time on a schooner that foundered in a violent storm on the western shore of Lake Michigan. Taken in for the winter by the hospitable Moore family of Waukegan, Illinois, Hannibal married their daughter Margretta the following spring, in 1857. Although three little girls were born to the young couple over the next several years, all died of diphtheria as infants or toddlers. In 1863 Hannibal joined the 17th Illinois Cavalry, in which he served, together with his brother-in-law William Moore, during the last years of the Civil War.

Hannibal and Margretta moved to Chicago after the war ended. Having already lost three children, they must have feared for the health of their fourth—a boy, Charles, born in 1864. Large northern cities were not healthy places in those days of epidemic disease, and Uncle Will—who had once lived near

Jacksonville while recuperating from a bout of tuberculosis—eventually persuaded them to move again, this time to Florida. A 28-foot sloop, the FAIRY BELLE, was purchased, refurbished, and outfitted for the trip. Tragedy was averted when the ship narrowly escaped incineration in the great Chicago fire of 1871, but the warehoused sails, spars, and rigging were destroyed. As soon as these could be replaced, the family and Uncle Will left the devastated city and set off down the Illinois River, bound for the Mississippi and the Gulf of Mexico.

After numerous adventures and mishaps the FAIRY BELLE made landfall on the west coast of Florida at Cedar Key in the summer of 1872. Warned by the locals not to sail south around the peninsula during hurricane season, the family sold the ship and crossed to the east coast on the recently completed Florida Railroad, settling first at Ankona Heights on Indian River, next at Jupiter, and finally (more or less permanently) on Lake Worth in 1873. Wittingly or no, they had arrived in what was perhaps the last extensive wilderness in the eastern United States.

Between Jupiter Inlet and the mouth of the Miami River, a distance of some eighty miles, not a single permanent settlement could be found anywhere along the ocean beach in the early 1870s. No desert island was lonelier, the coastline an unrelieved prospect of sand and dune vegetation as far as the eye could see. The pine flatwoods and swamps behind the beach, however, were favorite hunting grounds of the Seminoles, with whom the United States Army had fought a series of inconclusive wars, the last of which ended only fifteen years before the Pierces arrived on the lake. Although Hannibal liked the Indians and eventually came to trust them, Seminole hunting parties were prone to turn up unannounced at any time, causing nervousness among the women and children when the menfolk were away.

The lake itself was almost uninhabited, with but a single permanent resident in 1873. Twenty-one miles long and no more than a mile across at its widest point, it extended parallel to the coast and was only separated from the Atlantic Ocean by a narrow barrier beach. When the first settlers arrived, it was a pristine freshwater lake, fed by seepage from the eastern Everglades, just a few miles to the west. The Pierces settled on a large island near the south end of the lake, close to the portage (locally known as a "haulover") where small craft could be dragged across the sandy spit between lake and ocean. The settlers called it Hypoluxo Island, after the Seminole name for the lake itself.

Needless to say, pioneer life was difficult at first. Clouds of mosquitoes plagued the settlers in the summertime, and the dense subtropical jungle had to be cleared by hand for house construction and to plant crops. Fish and game were abundant, but cash to purchase powder and shot, tools, crockery, cloth, and other necessary manufactured items was in desperately short supply. Fortunately, some necessities, and a few creature comforts as well, came from the sea.

For the southeast Florida coast was a veritable graveyard of shipping. Southbound vessels headed for Key West, New Orleans, and the Gulf of Mexico sailed as close to the coast as possible to avoid the contrary northward current of the Gulf Stream. Without any lighthouse between Jupiter and Cape Florida, shipwrecks were commonplace events in the early 1870s, and quantities of lumber and cargo washed up on the beach as the wrecks broke up off shore. In fact, the Pierce house was built almost entirely from flotsam: the corner posts of heavy ship's timbers, the siding and floors from ship's planking. Many other useful items were also found along the ocean beach, remnants of ships wrecked in the hurricane of 1870, including scraps of brass and copper scavenged by young Charles (now a sturdy boy), which he sold to a shopkeeper in Titusville—160 miles away to the north—for pocket money.

Transportation was simple for the early pioneers: either you sailed or you walked. Even small children learned to handle boats competently on the lake, and boys at a surprisingly early age were entrusted with ferrying women, younger children, and cargo up and down the coast as needed. However, shank's mare was the only alternative when the wind was unfavorable, and settlers occasionally walked the beach from Lake Worth all the way to Miami, a distance of some sixty miles. Later the mail was carried by foot along the same stretch of coast by the legendary barefoot mailmen.

Shortly after the crew of a vessel wrecked in the hurricane of 1873 almost starved to death on the beach between New River and Biscayne Bay, the United States Life Saving Service began construction of five "houses of refuge," where shipwrecked sailors on Florida's east coast could at least be assured of shelter, food, and clothing. One of these, the Orange Grove House of Refuge, was sited just south of Lake Worth, and Hannibal was hired as its first keeper. Here it was that Gil's mother, Lillie Pierce, was born in 1876, but the family did not stay long. Margretta missed their house on the lake, so the family returned to Hypoluxo Island in 1877. Except for a brief episode when Hannibal was hired as keeper of the Biscayne Bay House of Refuge in 1882, they did not leave the lake again. Hannibal had finally settled down.

Life in the wilds of Florida was primitive in some respects, but the settlers were not illiterate, and their children did not grow up as uneducated savages. Margretta Pierce had been a schoolteacher back in Illinois, and she took pains with Charles' and Lillie's lessons; in today's parlance, they were home-schooled. Hannibal himself appears to have been a prolific letter writer, and his family in Maine dispatched regular packages of books and magazines that traveled down the coast by steamship and sailing skiff to the lake.[1] One imagines that these packages were eagerly anticipated, each book and magazine read with close attention, and their contents discussed after supper as adults rocked in the lamplight and children sat about on the

The Pierce homestead on Hypoluxo Island. *Left to right*: Margretta Pierce, Hannibal Pierce, Andrew Garnett (a neighbor), Ed Hamilton (another neighbor), Lillie Pierce (Gil's mother), and Charles Pierce (Uncle Charlie). Photographer unknown, ca. 1886.

ship-planked floors. Both Charles and Lillie grew up to be voracious readers and compulsive diarists, traits that were passed along to nephew and son long decades later.

Lacking playmates for much of her youth, Lillie grew up to be tough and self-reliant, learned to sail and shoot like a boy, and had many childhood adventures on the sea beach and the lake. Later, as one of the few marriageable young women in the region, she attracted much male attention. Among her admirers was one Frederick C. Voss, a steam engineer born in Maine to Danish immigrant parents. Fred first came to Lake Worth in 1888 and must have met Lillie when she was just a girl. The two were married in 1894, when Lillie was eighteen and Fred twenty-nine.

By that time, however, Henry Flagler's railroad had reached the lake, and life as the pioneers had once known it was gone for good. The west side of the lake was quickly developed as towns sprang up along the railroad in the pine flatwoods where Seminoles and pioneer boys had once hunted deer: Riviera, West Palm Beach, Lake Worth, Lantana, and Boynton.[2] Inlets were opened and enlarged, and navigation canals were dug, connecting the lake with the Intracoastal Waterway. Bridges were thrown across the lake at Lantana, Lake Worth, West Palm Beach, and elsewhere, linking towns along its western shoreline with oceanside developments. The twentieth century had arrived.

The Voss family first lived next to the Pierce homestead on Hypoluxo Island, but in 1909 Fred built a larger house at Hypoluxo, a small town between Lantana and Boynton on the adjacent

The house that Fred Voss built at Hypoluxo. The front screened porch was where Frederick, Walter, and Gil hung in their mackerel and pompano nets. Federal Highway is in the foreground. This house withstood many hurricanes. Photographer and date unknown.

mainland. He built well, and the house served as a neighborhood shelter during several storms, including the devastating 1928 hurricane. Two stories high, it faced Federal Highway—then a one-lane road surfaced with rock and shell—and backed on the lake. The screened front porch extended across the whole front of the house and afforded a welcome refuge from the still-prevalent hordes of summertime mosquitoes. When the insects were especially bad, a smudge pot filled with smoldering coconut husks was placed next to the front step, and a mosquito switch hung by the screen door. Family and visitors would stand in the pungent smoke for a few moments and use the switch to rid themselves of mosquitoes before stepping inside. Behind the house were a dock and several outbuildings, including a barn with stalls for livestock.

Gil was born in 1918, the youngest of Fred and Lillie's five children. His oldest siblings, Freda (Lillian Frederica) and Charlie (Charles Hannibal), were already young adults when Gil came along, but two brothers—Frederick and Walter—were only a few years older, and both were boon companions of his early years. Of the three younger boys, Frederick was the oldest and tended to be the leader, or at least the instigator, of any wild enterprise.

There are few recorded incidents from Gil's early childhood. By his own account it was a happy one, unmarked by tragedy or hardship, at least until the Depression. Margaret Garnett, a neighbor, recalled:

> Gilbert had a lot of imagination. He came to our house one day all dressed up. I pretended not to know who he was and he said, "I'm an Indian." Another time he was a pirate, then a soldier. When he came one day in his ordinary clothes, I still pretended not to know him. He said, "I'm just plain Gilbert today."[3]

Walter Voss (*left*) and Gilbert Voss in matching sailor suits. Studio photograph, ca. 1921.

Gil's elementary school days are completely undocumented. The Florida climate is not kind to paper, and the family seems not to have saved report cards, vaccination records, or any of the usual detritus of primary education. The only surviving fragment of his schoolboy literary efforts is an undated composition entitled "Going to Africa." Written in a firm but still immature hand, and displaying a fine contempt for punctuation, it suggests a Hannibal-like enthusiasm for voyaging and high adventure. Chapter 1, all of one paragraph long, begins and ends breathlessly:

> mr. anderson was sitting at his desk reading a book when suddenly the door opened and mr. ashly came in. a call to Africa he said. and i'm going. the man that sent it is hunting for the white mountain. he wants me and someone else to come and I'll take you with me.

A lifelong passion for reading was nurtured by Uncle Charlie—Lillie's older brother, by then postmaster at Boynton—who had one of the largest private libraries in town, including books by Jules Verne, G. A. Henty, H. Rider Haggard, and other popular authors. Uncle Charlie would loan the boy one volume at a time, on the condition that it be read cover to cover and discussed with him before another was loaned. The Pierce home in Boynton was also a sort of literary salon on Sunday afternoons, when Uncle Charlie would read aloud from recently typewritten pages of his account of pioneer life on the lake and discuss them with Lillie.[4] From them, young Gilbert learned the value of recording events and impressions soon after they occurred. From his father, a gifted raconteur, he also learned to tell a good story.

In 1924, when Gil was just six, Fred Voss and Lillie's cousin Walter Moore commissioned a 78-foot pleasure yacht to be built near Bath, Maine. Christened the DONNYGILL (for the owners' youngest sons, Donald and Gilbert), this was the family's principal source of income for the next five years. Chartered by wealthy parties from Long Island in the summertime and by clients from Palm Beach in the winter months, the DONNYGILL plied the Intracoastal Waterway, Chesapeake Bay, Long Island Sound, and other inshore waters from Florida to Maine. During these prosperous years the Voss children spent part of each

summer with relatives on the Maine coast, where the younger
boys ran barefoot and feral until the return trip to Florida and
the start of school in the fall.

Unfortunately, hard times followed. Fred lost his entire sav-
ings when the banks failed in 1929, and without moneyed clients to charter her, the DONNYGILL was laid up and eventually
sold. Because the family owned their home and had no mort-
gage to pay off, the Vosses made out better than many of their
neighbors in Hypoluxo, but money was scarce throughout Gil's
teenage years. The family farmed their lakeside property, raising
peppers, eggplants, grapefruit, bananas, and other produce that
they sold locally to buy groceries and other supplies. Everyone
pitched in, but hoeing and weeding are disagreeable chores for
restless boys, and none of them would grow up to be farmers.

Gil's enthusiasm for voyaging, undiminished by the usual
adolescent distractions, was indulged by his father, who built
the teenager an 18-foot wooden sharpie, the MOETUA. Flat-
bottomed, with a centerboard and two unstayed masts, sharpies
were ideal for lake and inshore sailing. Experienced young skip-
pers with a taste for adventure, however, could venture far beyond local waters. When Gil was seventeen, he and a high-school
friend set off by themselves on the MOETUA with fifteen dollars, some salt pork, flour, and a few canned goods to spend the
summer camping and sailing in the upper keys. The next summer
both youngsters sailed south again, this time as far as Key West.[5]

Shell collecting was another boyhood interest that Gil undertook with precocious energy and professionalism. There were a
number of serious collectors in the neighborhood while he was
growing up, including the McGintys (father and sons) of Boynton and the Lyman family of Lantana. Also living nearby was
Maxwell Smith, author of *East Coast Marine Shells*, an important
reference volume for prewar shell collectors. Smith was not a
beachcomber seeking trophy specimens, but a dedicated ama-

Gil on vacation in Maine. The Voss children spent summers with relatives on the
Maine coast while the DONNYGILL was cruising Long Island Sound and other
northern waters. Photographer unknown, ca. 1928.

teur conchologist who scoured marine habitats for mollusks of all kinds and communicated with scientists at the big eastern museums and universities about unusual discoveries. He probably taught the teenager to use scientific terminology, to label specimens correctly, and to classify his growing collection on taxonomic principles. Gil must have shown some promise, because Smith recruited him to help dredge for mollusks at the south end of Lake Worth in 1935, an early experience in biological inventory that netted more than 360 species.[6]

Gil graduated from Lake Worth High School in 1937. Despite improving economic conditions, the family's circumstances were

The State of Florida, showing places mentioned in the text. Details of the Lake W region (between Jupiter and Boca Raton) are shown on the next map.

such that college was not an option. For a seafaring young man without military ambitions, the choices for employment at the time were pretty much limited to the Merchant Marine or fishing. Gil tried his hand at both before the war, but this narrative concerns fishing, and it is now time to step back and let the fisherman tell it in his own words.

The text that follows is essentially unchanged from Gil's last typescript, incorporating only minor edits, some of which he had already marked. At the request of the University Press of Florida, however, I have inserted short headnotes to his chapters as well as endnotes on various relevant topics. Of course, any errors that might be introduced by this material or by the glossary that follows the main text are mine alone.

Robert S. Voss
Tenafly, New Jersey

Introduction

This is the story of my Florida, the Florida I grew up in and learned to love. It is mostly about fishermen, the people of the east and west coasts whom I knew best, the ones who colored my life in my early years and who, along with my seafaring family, gave me my appreciation for the sea and its denizens. That I became a naturalist and an oceanographer was due to a quirk of fate. I might just as easily have stayed a sportsfishing guide and a charterboat captain. If I had, this book would never have been written.

Many changes have taken place since these events occurred. New fishing methods have been introduced, new types of boat have been developed, some whole fisheries have disappeared. Crystal River and Flamingo are no longer recognizable as they were just forty years ago. But the people remain. Fishermen are fishermen: unique, hardworking, hard drinking, colorful in speech, philosophical in disposition.

During my early years I was fortunate to see and participate in a number of different fisheries, more than most fishermen have seen. Others may have known the fisheries better, but those who did have failed to record their experiences. The events described here, as far-fetched as some may seem, are all true, and most were written down at the time they happened, for I was even then experimenting with writing. They portray a Florida little known today. I hope that in their reading you can get a feeling for the Florida that has passed. If I have spent more time talking about fishermen and less about fishing in some cases, it is because I find people more interesting than fish and fishermen more interesting than most people. I hope that you agree.

1

Prohis and Fish Wardens

Nowhere in the country was Prohibition ignored like it was in Florida. Rivers of illicit booze flowed through the speakeasies of Miami and the oceanfront estates of Palm Beach, but all of it had seeped into the state clandestinely by boat, run in at night onto lonely beaches or through mangrove-choked inlets to waiting trucks on shore. Boat captains ran the risk of running liquor past the Coast Guard, the well-to-do shelled out big bucks for drinks, and organized crime pocketed huge profits. For younger boys in small fishing communities along the southeast coast, rum-running was a nightly spectator sport; for older boys there was money to be made—if they didn't get caught.

R.S.V.

I wouldn't say that native Floridians disregarded or flouted the law, they just felt that some laws were wrong and ignored them. This attitude generally was directed toward laws that prohibited them from doing what had always been done, like making and drinking 'shine during Prohibition, or rum-running, or digging turtle eggs, or net-fishing in Lake Worth. Prohis (Prohibition officers, pronounced "pro-highs") and Isaak Walton League fish wardens were scorned by nearly everyone and were circumvented whenever possible. The LAW in Palm Beach County was Sheriff Bob Baker, and he was respected and obeyed. Bob Baker did not have much use for prohis or Isaak Walton League wardens either. After all, he was a cracker too.[1]

Fishing and rum-running were often synonymous. The fishermen knew the coast, its inlets and network of waterways, better than anyone else, including the prohis and their government confederates, the Coast Guard. I was too young for any action in those days, but my brothers were teenagers when a rum runner ran Boynton Inlet with a Coast Guard boat in hot pursuit. Both the rum runner and the Coast Guard ran aground on the shoals inside the inlet, but the rummy got free by heaving over the side most of its cargo of Scotch, which was done up in lots of three bottles each, neatly sewn in burlap. The rummy then ran off into the mangroves and the Coast Guard lost them.

The sacks of Scotch floated for a while and then sank, distributed by the incoming tide all over the south end of the lake. Word of the bonanza spread like wildfire, and next morning my brothers in their outboard were searching the lake with a dozen other boys, diving up the sacks in the clear water. The prohis were roaming the roads by car and helplessly watching the activity in the lake. They never caught on to the rum runners, who were buying back the sacks at $10 each as fast as they were brought ashore.

Another day a Coast Guard 75-footer was chasing a big rum runner up the lake. The Lantana bridge was a swing-draw high enough for the rummy to go under but too low for the patrol boat. At the foot of the lake the patrol boat began blowing for the bridge and we heard her repeated blasts, becoming more strident as she neared the bridge. The draw was still swinging as the rummy roared underneath. The draw was barely open when there was a BOOM from the patrol boat firing her one-pounder through the draw. The bridge tender threw himself flat as another shell screamed by.

The patrol boat roared through the open space, creating a tremendous wake, but she suddenly lost headway and began to drift. Just as the rummy ran through the draw, her crew had

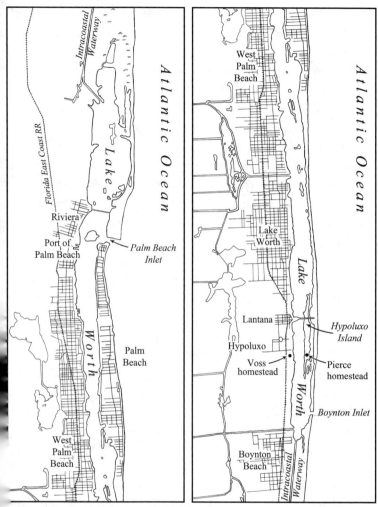

Lake Worth in the mid-1930s. The left-hand panel shows the north end of the lake, the right-hand panel the south end.

thrown over a section of mackerel net, which wrapped itself around the blades and shafts of the patrol boat's propellers, putting the pursuers temporarily out of commission. Frustrated, the men at the gun continued firing at the rummy until she was beyond range, unscathed.

In fact, Coast Guard boats were not fast enough to catch a rummy and never did until one broke down in a chase. It was immediately converted into the Coast Guard's first fast picket boat. Years later, I was in charge of her at Miami during our first year in World War II. She had a 350-horsepower Murray Tregurtha engine but with stops on the throttle. When I took them off she was the fastest picket boat in the fleet.[2]

But this book is about fishing, and Lake Worth was filled with fish that the Isaak Walton League seemed determined to preserve only for the sportsfishermen, or so everyone thought. In the fall, as the first northeasters came along, bluefish and Spanish mackerel invaded the lake around the two inlets. Commercial fishermen in small boats fished for both, using a strip of white cloth for the mackerel and a no. 6 Wilson spoon or a strip of white pork rind for the blues. The small boats were so thick in the steamship channel at the Port of Palm Beach that the Merchants and Miners Transportation Company and Bull Line freighters occasionally ran one down.

Besides these migratory fish there were sea trout, big snook, and redfish for the taking with trolling or casting gear. Mullet and sand perch abounded but could only be caught by cast net or seine. The big black mullet was a staple fish on the lake, and anyone with a cast net could easily catch enough for supper in a few minutes.

Sand perch (*Diapterus plumieri*) are large, flat, silvery fish that were highly prized locally as pan fish. The common name is confusing because this fish is known elsewhere as mojarra or broad shad, while on Biscayne Bay the fish they call sand perch is a long, round, ugly creature with an enormous mouth (*Diplectrum formosum*). Sand perch (or striped mojarra) were occasionally caught by cast-netters, but commercially they were taken in gill nets.

And then there were pompano. This highly overrated fish brought anywhere from twenty-five cents to a dollar a pound to the fisherman. A few people fished them commercially with hook and line and made a few dollars a day, but pompano were mainly caught with pompano gill nets or trammel nets.

Most native Floridians, and especially fishermen, have little culinary regard for pompano. Absolutely fresh, practically still flapping, and pan-broiled in a little rendered-out white bacon fat, it is delicious. Iced, it loses its flavor, but it has thick, white meat with only a few easily removable bones and a delicate texture. With no fishy flavor, it makes an excellent, tasteless base upon which to pour or ladle various French sauces and condiments so that the poor pompano is no longer recognizable as fish. So-called gourmets now pay exorbitant prices to "ooh" and "ah" over the sauce and praise the chef for his beautifully prepared *fish*. But there are few fish so beautifully sleek, silvery and firm as a pompano, and at a dollar apiece their beauty is even more dramatic. Pompano live along the open coast or in estuaries, feeding on crabs and clams in shallow, sandy flats. When alarmed by a passing boat they have the odd habit of jumping at high speed, flat on their sides, out of the water and toward the wake or boat, often jumping into the boat itself.

All sorts of curious tales are told about this strange behavior; fishermen are full of them, and two are known to me personally. One pompano jumped through the port hole of our charter yacht and fell on the galley floor. Another time, my father was taking a friend to Palm Beach in his steam launch to have a boil lanced, when a pompano jumped into the boat, hit the boil on the man's shoulder, burst it open, and fell to the deck. This ended the trip to the doctor and afforded an evening meal for the patient.

This typical behavior also originated a new type of fishing. Several of the conchs at Riviera built long, slender flatties, set up poles bow and stern, and stretched old mackerel nets in between. In the quiet of the early morning or late afternoon they towed these flatties behind high-speed sea skiffs at 18 or 20 knots over the shallows around the inlet. If schools of pompano were on the flats feeding, they showered into the wake as the boats raced back and forth across the shoals, the fish hitting the webbing and falling into the skiffs. On a good series of runs 50 to 100 pounds of pompano could be caught, and as the net was not "set" and was never in the water, it was all perfectly legal.

Pompano are also attracted to lights. In the early days a gas lantern suspended over a small boat anchored on the flats might result in a half-full boat of fish by morning.

But we were discussing the law and fishing. The fishermen began to run into the law when the Isaak Walton League succeeded in getting a law passed to prevent gill-netting and purse or beach seining in the inland waters of Florida, specifically Lake Worth and Indian River, or within 500 yards of an inlet in the open ocean. Few fishermen paid much attention to the new law, and most of them continued to set their gill nets for pompano and sand perch. The League then hired its own wardens, deputized to make arrests. They had fast outboard boats and powerful searchlights. The nets' cork floats showed up like strings of buoys, easily seen with the lights, and arrests began to roll in. The game had begun.

Cork lines were soon changed to heavy cords, and corks were replaced by slender wooden floats that barely showed above the surface. With padded transoms, the fisherman hid in the mangroves until the coast was clear, silently set his net, and returned to the mangroves. With luck, the net soaked for several hours and was then drawn up and taken ashore to pick out the fish. It was risky business, however; if he were caught, both boat and net were confiscated, and the fisherman was fined or jailed, perhaps both.

One night my brothers devised a new ploy.

The warden was cruising the south end of the lake. Walter started up his outboard and ran across to the other shore. This drew the warden away, and Frederick set his net a mile to the northward. The warden cruised the south end, flashing his light across the water looking for the telltale floats on the net that he knew was there. For two hours he searched, while Frederick, with his hand on the cork line, felt the fish hitting the net. Then the warden cut off his motor to listen. In the dead of the night he suddenly heard the sound of net leads being pulled across the stern of a boat. The outboard roared to life, the light came on, and he saw what he thought was a net being hauled into a boat. He ran down alongside.

"I've got you!" he shouted. "You're under arrest."

"What for?" asked Walter.

"Don't give me that stuff. For illegal fishing in the lake." He flashed the light into the boat. There was no net and no fish. All that was in the bottom of the boat was a length of line with a dozen leads on it that Walter had been drawing back and forth across the transom.

With a curse the warden started up again and ran north, flashing his light back and forth across the lake. But by now Frederick had picked up and gone ashore with a hundred pounds of pompano and almost as many sand perch.

The Lantana bridge tender had been giving the fellows a hard time and informing the wardens about their activities. One rainy, blustery night Frederick decided to get even. About midnight, well bundled up, he and a friend, Gus Hagg, approached the bridge in a rowboat with an outboard motor, a light held aloft on a bamboo pole, and with running lights showing. Blast after blast of a fog horn finally woke the bridge tender. Putting on his clothes and rain gear he closed the gates, put the long crank into the lock, raised it, and began the long job of walking the crank round. Wind and rain lashed him. The bridge was slippery and the going hard. Finally the bridge was open.

Gus lowered the pole with the light, Frederick sped up the motor, and the bridge tender went to the side to record the name of the boat. The tender took one look, started yelling, grabbed the crank out of the center of the span, and threw it at them. It missed and fell into the lake. Now the tender had no crank, the bridge was open, and there was no way to get back to his house for a spare. Revenge was sweet.[3]

The following account may be apocryphal, but it has been around a long time and seems worth retelling.

Up on Indian River a mullet fisherman was caught with net and fish. Conviction meant confiscation of net and boat, plus a jail term. He hired a lawyer.

When the defense's time came, a zoologist from a Florida university was called and qualified as an expert witness.

"What kind of animals have gizzards?" the lawyer asked.

The zoologist answered promptly. "Birds."

"Do any other vertebrate animals have gizzards?"

"No."

The lawyer took a plate from the table, carried it over to the zoologist, and whipped off the cover.

"What are these?" he asked.

The zoologist examined the contents carefully and even cut one open.

"They are gizzards."

The lawyer approached the bench.

"Your honor, the expert witness has just testified that only birds have gizzards. These gizzards were just removed from some of the mullet taken by the defendant. I submit that on the evidence given, these came from birds, not fish, and request that the case be dismissed."

The judge laughed. He was a local judge and had eaten many a dish of mullet gizzards.

"I find the defendant not guilty. Case dismissed."

Florida has the only mullet birds in the world.

2

~~~~~~~~~~~~~~~~~~~~~~

"Power in de hold, mon!"

Nets are among the oldest known ways to catch fish, and many species (like mullet, which will not take bait) cannot be caught any other way. Several kinds of nets were once used in Florida waters, including gill nets, beach seines, and cast nets. Back in the day fishermen made and repaired their own nets. Net making and net mending were crucial occupational skills, and both were everyday activities along the waterfronts of small towns up and down the Florida coast. During the off season nets were dried on racks before being folded away for storage, and old photographs of Florida shorelines often have racks of drying nets in the background.

Gill nets were the most important equipment used by the artisanal inshore fisheries described in this book. These were rectangular nets—much longer than they were high—supported at the top by a head rope provided with floats (the cork line) and weighted at the bottom by a foot rope provided with sinkers (the lead line). The position of the net in the water column could be altered by adjusting the ratio of floats to weights. Heavily weighted gill nets that sank to the bottom in deep water, with the cork line submerged, were known as stab nets.

The gill nets used in the midcentury mackerel fishery of southeast Florida were usually from 250 to 900 yards long with webbing made of no. 6 or no. 9 cotton twine. A single length of gill net was known as a shot (presumably from its action as it went overboard from a boat traveling at speed). Gill nets were remarkably effective when expertly used: a 500-yard-long net could capture up to 10,000 pounds of fish.

Gill nets capture fish by entanglement. A fish is caught when it penetrates the mesh beyond its gill covers but is too thick at midbody to pass completely through; as it tries to free itself, the twine slips behind the gill covers and prevents escape. Gill nets are size-selective because small fish can swim right through the mesh, whereas most fish that are too large to penetrate the mesh do not become entangled. Therefore, gill nets are woven to catch particular target species, hence mackerel nets, mullet nets, et cetera. The mackerel nets described in Gil's accounts typically had a mesh size between 3⅛ and 3⅜ inches (stretched), which would mostly have taken fish about 15 to 20 inches long. Gill nets were sometimes set to "soak" in likely places and catch fish unattended, but mullet, bluefish, and mackerel were more frequently taken in so-called runaround gill nets, set in a circular or oblong pattern to enclose a school of fish, which were then frightened into the net by various means.[1]

R.S.V.

Just north of the city of West Palm Beach, about opposite the in-let, is the town of Riviera Beach. Today it is pronounced in the French fashion, *Ri-vi-er-a*, but in the 1930s it was just plain *Ri-vier-a*, as it is today to the natives and old-timers. It was also known as Conch Town, because most of its inhabitants were conchs or out-islanders from the Bahamas. The men were tanned, dark-skinned and weathered, but the girls were often real beauties. The conchs came from Abaco, Eleuthera, Exeuma, Governor's

Harbour, and Spanish Wells. They spoke conch, the singsong Caribbean-accented Cockney English of the true out-islanders, and they were fishermen and boat builders.

When the wind was blowing fresh from the east and the seas were rough, they squatted on the wharves, fisherman style, talking in their almost-unintelligible island dialect, or mended nets (although most of this work was usually done by the girls and women), or worked on their boats, or hung about the boat yards giving superfluous advice to the builders of the big lapstreak sea skiffs. When the wind laid and the seas ran down, they net-fished for Spanish mackerel, bluefish, and pompano, or handlined for kingfish (or king mackerel, as they are called today). Their big, fast Palm Beach skiffs were famous on the coast.

The first sea skiffs were brought down from New Jersey in the late 1800s. They had lapstreak hulls of white cedar or juniper with narrow, steamed-oak ribs and were copper-riveted. The Jersey skiffs were narrow-sterned, with a narrow flat bottom amidships and with a box garboard aft. All the first sea skiffs were launched from the beach, and the net crews consisted of five to six men, the captain at the tiller or steering oar and the others at the long oars. The narrow flat bottoms let the boats beach upright, and no better surf boats were ever built. When engines were introduced they were widely adopted. Built as these skiffs were, it was almost impossible to broach one to in a following sea. When running the bar, the fishermen sometimes dropped the tiller and let the boat find its own position in the surf.

When the conchs adopted the Jersey skiffs they broadened the sterns, put a slight reverse hook in the bottom, and made a flat transom. Now, with the addition of more powerful, faster engines, the Palm Beach skiffs came into their own: great surf boats, fast, dry, but no longer launched off the beach. They became famous on the coast as net boats.

During the Depression my brother Frederick acquired an old Jersey sea skiff with a slow, heavy-duty engine. The hull had

Net-drying racks and sea skiff next to docks and fish house at Riviera Beach. Essentially similar scenes, complete with barefoot urchins, were commonplace up and down the east coast of Depression-era Florida. Photo by C. C. Foster, 1939; State Archives of Florida.

squat-boards around the stern at the water's edge to keep her from squatting in the water at full speed. She was an old boat, and the fastenings were so loose that in a seaway she had to be pumped regularly and often. Twenty-four hours at the dock and she would tighten up and not leak a drop.

My introduction to commercial fishing as a boy was in OLD WHEEZY, as we called her. During the summer we would go out through Boynton Inlet. At that time it was still rated as a drainage cut, not an inlet, and there was a shallow ledge in the mouth. On the ebb tide you actually dropped a few inches running the inlet, like going over a dam.

Once outside, we would run out to one of the deep reefs in about 40 to 60 feet. The water was gin clear, and I could watch the heavy lead sinker and white bait as they sank slowly down among the rocks, big sponges, and sea whips. If the fishing was good it was only a few minutes before the line would give a jerk as a fish took the bait and made off with it. The handlines were hard-laid and tarred, and cotton fishermen's gloves were needed to handle them. Sometimes the fish was too big, and after a fight the line or the leader broke or the hook straightened out. Those fish that came to the surface and were hauled aboard were grouper, red ones with mottled sides, black- or gray-and-white ones, beautifully colored ones with yellow fins, or gorgeous spotted rock hinds. Mutton snapper and African pompano, amberjacks, and others also came flopping aboard. Occasionally a big barracuda would chop a fish in two, leaving only the head. And not infrequently a great, long hammerhead shark would come on the scene. If we were hauling in a fish, the shark would usually get it.

If we were lucky we might come upon a loggerhead turtle asleep at the surface, or feeding on Portuguese men-of-war, chomping slowly away with its eyes closed. A sleeping turtle is hard to approach closely enough to gaff, but if one has been feeding on men-of-war, the poison of the stinging cells is discharged in the turtle's stomach and partially or completely paralyzes the

animal. Sometimes we would find one with a single flipper para-
lyzed but more often two, both on the same side. Trying to escape, the turtle would spin round and round, unable to swim in
a straight line. Most people believe that only the green turtle is
good eating, but a loggerhead turtle of no more than about 50
pounds and fat around the flippers is every bit as good and perhaps better. Its tenderness depends largely upon the butchering
technique.

Occasionally (this was in the late 1920s and early 1930s), a long,
slender, bluish fish with a big dorsal fin would trail in our wake.
We had no idea that these creatures would soon make south Florida world famous, and we did not even know what to call them.
Some people were calling them spearfish, others sailfish.

During the Depression we suffered along with our neighbors,
and it is still a wonder to me how my father fed his family. When
the fishing was poor, or it was too rough to go out through the
inlet, and when cast-netting for mullet in the lake was unsuccessful, we had little meat and were often reduced to eating
fried-out salt pork or sowbelly. To make it seem less repulsive,
my mother would serve it one day as pork, another as steak, the
next as chicken or turkey. One day a neighbor's son rode over on
his bike. As he stood in the yard he asked what we were having
for dinner.

"We're having turkey," my mother replied.

His eyes lit up. "Turkey! Do you think I could eat with you
today?"

"Why certainly, come on in."

As we asked to have the turkey passed and he saw the fried
sowbelly his face fell, but he then ate with gusto what he would
probably have had at home.

"I ate over at the Vosses,'" he told his family when he got
back, "and we had turkey for dinner. It sure was good."

All the rest of the Depression years, people in Hypoluxo ate their sowbelly under a variety of names but never again as salt pork.

My father was a Downeaster from Maine and used to tell of how the Newfoundlanders salted down barrels of cod to carry them over the winter. One fish was always nailed to the bottom of the barrel, and if the fish ran out before the winter was over, they rubbed their boiled potatoes on the last cod to give them some flavor. It followed the old saying, "Fish and potatoes, the fat of the land, those that don't like them can starve and be damned."

We tried it with loggerhead turtle but without nailing a piece to the bottom. The turtle was carefully cut up and salted down in a small keg, which was kept in the pantry. At first it was pretty good, a welcome relief from salt pork or "Depression turkey," but after a few weeks the meat got tougher and tougher, and despite every tenderizing method my mother knew, it finally got too tough to chew, and the rest was thrown away. We never tried salt turtle again.

Still with OLD WHEEZY, my brothers turned to kingfishing. Kingfish usually came down the coast with the first of the northeasters and schooled at various places along the coast from Palm Beach to Miami. One of the biggest concentrations was off the old Barbara Hutton estate in south Palm Beach. Boats came from as far away as Panama City in the upper Gulf of Mexico to fish in the fleet. Up to two hundred boats might be fishing the school at one time, all going in a big circle to keep clear of one another.

This was a handline fishery. You took a full coil of no. 10 leader wire, or piano wire as it was called, cut it in two, wrapped a stiff hook on one end, and made the other end fast to the gunwale of the boat with a couple of feet of handline. Midship of the boat was the fish box with an upright board in the middle; the board was notched with a deep V, across which a heavy wire was strung as an unhooker.

The bait was a strip of white belly, two baits from each fish. The blunt end was stuck on the short, projecting end of the leader wire just ahead of the hook, and the point of the hook was shoved through the strip. Hook and bait were then thrown free and the 150 feet of wire were run out. The fisherman stood by the side and jerked the wire rhythmically. When a king struck, the wire was brought in by wide swings of the arms with the wire caught in a half turn of each gloved hand. It was hard work, for a big kingfish of 35 to 40 pounds is a real tussle. School kings ran 10 to 12 pounds. When the fish came over the side, the fisherman swung it through the air and over the unhooker, where the hook caught on the heavy wire, and the fish fell off into the box. It sounds simple, but kingfishing was an art.

Catastrophe might strike at any time if porpoises arrived on the scene. Immediately yells and curses could be heard throughout the fleet as fish after fish was caught by the hungry porpoises, which bit the fish off clean just behind the gills, leaving only the head for the luckless fisherman. Porpoise attacks would send the whole school of kings to the bottom, where they stayed until the porpoises left.

Kingfish only brought 10 to 12 cents a pound. When the real run began, the price dropped to 6 and then to 2 cents; then the fish house would close down.

Several times we were caught with a load of fish and no sale. We would stand by the side of the road in front of our house and sell a ten-pound fish for a quarter. Often there were no takers. On occasion we would put them in our pickup truck and peddle them from door to door in Lake Worth for a quarter apiece. And some people would refuse to buy unless the fish were cleaned for them. Often whole truckloads were given to the fire station for distribution to the needy.

Bluefishing was another matter. Bluefish were caught by trolling with a lead squid jig just outside the surf, where the blues ran. This fishing was known as squidding. One day Frederick invited a friend to go bluefishing with him. They found the fish down off Lake Worth just outside rather dangerous surf. The friend pulled blues with glee.

"This is great, Fred, let me know when you are going again, and I'll come along."

Just then a big rogue sea made up offshore, hit the sea skiff, and rolled her completely over and back up again. The friend was thrown out along with most of the bluefish, and he swam ashore. Frederick threw the anchor over, brought the boat head to the combers shoreward of the break, pumped her out, and tried to start the engine. He couldn't get so much as a sputter out of it. The fire extinguisher was filled with pyrene and he squirted it all over the wires, plugs, and distributor and hit the starter again. The engine roared to life.[2]

"Swim out and I'll pull you on board," he called to his erstwhile companion.

"And you can go to hell before I'll get back in that boat," the friend yelled from the beach. He then picked up two of the largest fish that had washed ashore and headed up to the beach road to hitch a ride home. Fishermen are born, not made.

As economic conditions improved, Walter and Frederick bought a new, fast sea skiff, the VIKING, powered with a big eight-cylinder Pierce Arrow car engine with a hot manifold. She had been locally built by Horace Sweeton, a Tennessee hillbilly just starting out in the boat-building business. When the boat was finished she turned out to have a big, high, forward-slanting bow and a low, broad stern but with nothing in between. Horace took one look at her outside the shed and shook his head. "She looks like she swapped legs with a killdee and got cheated out of her ass."

But she could go to windward in a head sea better than any Riviera-built skiff, and she was dry. We now went gill-netting for mackerel, bluefish, and pompano. The big nets were expensive, so my brothers got financial backing from the Hudgins Fish Company, with the agreement that the costs would be paid back by selling the catch exclusively to the company.

The webbing, cork and lead lines, corks, and leads, with balls of hanging-in twine and net needles, were distributed in one corner of our long screened-in front porch. Five hundred yards of mackerel net and 300 yards of pompano net were then hung in, with the tedious job of stringing leads and corks on the lines being turned over to me. I also filled the net needles and occasionally was permitted to try my hand at hanging in the webbing. By the time both nets were finished, I was skilled at all of it.

High school was in session when the mackerel fishing started, but I got off every day possible to go gill-netting. Mackerel run in the winter time, and I spent days on end dressed in oilskins, sea boots, and sou'wester, for gill-netting is a wet business.

The easy netting was done in shallow water just outside the breakers. The gill net was laid out in the stern with a long line fastened to the lead line, while the other end was bent onto a bucket, which was kept alongside the person running the engine amidships. A handline was fastened to the cork line with a white cloth for a lure. The boat was run down the shore with the handline out, held by Walter at the engine controls. Two or three strikes from mackerel were enough to make a set.

Frederick stood in the bow on a small deck over the cuddy, steering with the steering lines. When Walter yelled "Strike!" Frederick would give the deck a couple of bangs with his boot as a signal to open the throttle and throw the bucket over the side. The bucket grabbed the water and the net shot out over the transom with the sound of a machine gun as corks and leads hit the stern. Frederick would then make a quick turn offshore and back on the boat's track to go around and offshore of the supposed school. As the end of the net approached, he pulled the boat around again, forming another hook in the end of the net. The boat was now run back and forth inshore of the net with Walter slamming the gunwales with the sweep oar and stamping on the deck to frighten the fish into the net. With a good catch the cork line began to sink. The boat was now brought around to the end of the net, the bunch of corks forming a float was picked up, and the slow process of hauling in the net and picking out the fish began.

If the fish were not too numerous, they were all picked out of the net as it came over the side and thrown into the fish bins on either side of the engine box. If the catch was a big one, however, the net might be hauled in and the boat run to the fish dock, where the fish could be picked out and iced down immediately. One good set might bring in 6,000 pounds of mackerel, a full load.

The conchs at Riviera were the expert mackerel fishermen. They spread out all over the ocean during good weather, and with their big fast boats, often powered with twin Gray or Chrysler Marine engines, they could run up to 30 knots light with three shots of net aboard. Conchs could even smell mackerel and bluefish from the oil on the surface when the fish were feeding. I have seen a conch gill-netter set his net simply because he saw a seagull dip toward the water ahead of him—and come up with a net loaded with fish.

The real fun and excitement to me was night fishing, when the schools were sighted by fire in the water.[3] This fishing was done only in the dark of the moon. If the moon was still up in the early evening, we would pull into Jupiter Inlet, if the bar was passable, build a fire on the beach, make coffee, and cook a mackerel or two in a bucket of seawater. When the fish were done they were broken open along the backbone, butter was melted on them, and canned milk was poured over the white meat. Hot and juicy; I have never eaten such fish before or since. Of course, the setting might have had something to do with it, and I was young.

The Voss brothers and a friend relax after a long day on the water. *Left to right*: Frederick Voss, Walter Voss, Gilbert Voss, and Jack Williams. Photographer unknown, ca. 1938.

As the moon went down the boats all started up, ran the bar, and spread out over the ocean looking for fire in the water. When a set was made at night, the fish were scared into the net by flashing the surface with a spotlight mounted in the bow. Picking up at night was done as fast as possible, because the lanterns on the floats and the flashing of the light attracted sharks, which not only took fish but also tore great holes in the net. On the run back to the fish house, coffee was made on the hot manifold and whole mackerel were broiled on its hot surface.

The mackerel run started with fish bringing 10 to 12 cents a pound, but as with kingfish, the price soon dropped to 6 cents, then 3 cents, 2 cents, 1 cent, and then the boats were told not to go back out. When the fish house closed before a boat got back to the dock, 6,000 pounds of fish went overboard or were given away.

Pompano were the prize fish, as they brought from 25 cents to a dollar a pound. They were caught with large-mesh pompano nets fished in shallow water, like mackerel. Pompano were fished on calm days. The boat ran along as close as possible to the beach at about half speed. When a pompano or two skipped in the wake, the throttle was pushed open, the bucket tossed over, and around went the boat to take in the school.

Pompano like to lurk around sand bars near inlets. This got us in bad with the hook-and-line fishermen casting off the jetties, and a law was soon passed that prohibited net fishing within 500 yards of inlets. Often this distance was misjudged, sometimes the current carried the net inside the limits, while a few fishermen simply ignored the rule. For whatever reason, if a net came within casting distance, the jetty fishermen, not realizing how heavy a net was, would cast their lures into the net, attempting to drag it ashore. Usually they wound up losing their lures and a considerable amount of line.

But all was not well in our last year of commercial fishing. Prices went down for mackerel, pompano were scarce, and the bluefish were small. In late fall the price for mackerel rose, but the shallow-water schools were few and small. For some reason the mackerel were offshore in deep water. This meant stab netting, which was hard work.

In stab netting, first practiced at Riviera by the conchs and later introduced by them to the New Jersey fishermen, the gill nets were heavy-leaded so that they sank quickly to the bottom in 60 to 100 feet or more. On the end of the cork line was a long line with a cork raft with a lantern fastened to it.

Stab netting was done at night in the dark of the moon, when the fish could be located by the fire in the water as they darted from the path of the boat. The bucket was heaved over, the net was run out in a straight line, and the boat slowed down while the lantern was put over. Then the boat was run back and forth inshore of the net while the spotlight was flashed back and forth across the surface, scaring the fish into the net. Then came the long, hard job of hauling the net back up by hand, a couple of feet at a time. Each boat had a light rigged above the engine amidships so that the fishermen could see to pick out the fish. Pulling the net up from 100 feet was backbreaking work. If there was a little sea running, it helped, for one pulled on the downward roll and held on the upward roll, so that the rolling helped to haul the net. I did not like stab netting.

One evening just before dark the mackerel fleet got under way from the docks at Riviera. Each boat had its shot of net carefully piled in the stern, cork line on one side, lead line on the other. The boats lay alongside the dock as the fishermen in their sea boots jumped aboard their individual sea skiffs. The Riviera conchs never dreamed of warming up their engines. As each two-man crew jumped aboard, one went to the steering lines or side tiller, the other to the engine controls. Bow and stern lines were cast off. At a signal from the helmsman, the engines were started up. The helmsman yelled, "Power in de hold, mon!" Both throttles were pulled full open, and the boat shot away from the dock in a streak of spray, on top and planing before it reached the end of the pier, headed for the inlet.

Fish had been seen off Jupiter, so the fleet headed north. Moonset was at about 10:00 pm, so many of the boats went into Jupiter Inlet and either anchored or beached gently on the sand bar on the north bank. We built a fire of cabbage palmetto frond stems, made coffee, and boiled a mackerel we had caught coming in.

As the moon set behind the pines, and the Jupiter lighthouse sent its beam across the water, the fleet came to life, and the boats raced for the open sea. Offshore, the water was suddenly filled with fire. Frederick turned the VIKING parallel to the shore, Walter heaved the bucket overboard, and the net ran out over the transom. All around us boats were setting their nets. We stopped to put over the light, and then Frederick turned around and began flashing the spotlight across the water while we stamped on the deck with our sea boots, and I slammed the sweep oar across the gunwales. After a few minutes of flashing out the net, we turned and picked up the light.

We began hauling in. The end of the net had not reached the surface before we knew that something was wrong. We could feel heavy jerks and tugs on the webbing that were not made by mackerel. Off to starboard we heard loud curses from one boat, then from another. When the net came up it was filled with mackerel, lots of mackerel, but for every mackerel there was a shark, seemingly enormous in the faint light, tearing at the mackerel and the webbing: a milling inferno of sharks. It soon became a tug-of-war between us and the sharks. Great holes appeared, dozens of them. There was no question of picking out as we hauled in; our only concern was to get that net away from the sharks while there was still anything left of it.

The crews of all the boats were yelling. Everyone had sharks. We pulled net as we had never pulled before. Sometimes there was only the lead line and cork line with no net between. On we hauled, desperately now. Around the boat sharks were milling about, bumping the sides. We got the last of the net on board and sat back, exhausted. Over the side sharks were as thick as the mackerel had been. I picked up the sweep oar and hit at them, only to have a shark bite the blade and nearly jerk it out of my hand.

"Let's get out of here," Frederick said, "before they start chewing on the boat. Douse those two lights."

The lights went out, but the sharks still rubbed and bumped into the thin, white cedar planking. Walter started the engine and put it in forward. There were several clunks as the propeller blades apparently hit a shark but did no damage. Frederick eased ahead, and we slowly cleared the sharks immediately around us. When we were clear he stomped on the deck, Walter opened the throttle, and we headed for home. All around us the fleet was dousing lights and getting under way for Riviera.

It was a half-scared but glum fleet that tied up to the dock that night. The fish were picked out, weighed in, and loaded into the fish house, but the nets were a mess. We loaded ours into our pickup truck to take home to repair. The next day we overhauled the net and looked at one another. It was ruined. In 300 yards of net there must have been 500 holes, some that could be mended, some that needed patching, and some big enough to drive a car through.

Frederick and Walter went in to get their check for the fish at Hudgins Fish Company in West Palm Beach. One of the Hudgins brothers asked them about the night's fishing and the condition of their net. When they had told him, he asked them to sit down.

"Listen, fellows. You two are not conchs. You'll never really make a decent living at commercial fishing. We keep most of the conchs in Riviera year-in-year-out at a living wage, no more. Most of them have credit with us or one of the other fish companies, get loans for new boats and nets, sell to us, and are more or less in debt all their lives. Get out now, while you can."

He reached into his drawer and pulled out a checkbook. "You still owe us a little for the cost of your nets. Your boat is your own." He figured for a moment or two, wrote out a check, and handed it to Frederick.

"Here, take this. This is what we'll give you for your nets and your boat. It's a good price, as you can see. With that you can get into some other line of boating."

Frederick and Walter looked at the check. Frederick folded it and put it in his pocket. They got up and shook hands with Mr. Hudgins.

"You've done the wise thing, fellows, you'll not regret it. Good luck to the both of you."

A few months later Frederick bought an old sailfishing boat, the FUN, renamed it the LUCKY LADY, and found his life profession. For me it opened a new world of fishing.

3

Cap Knight and the Bear

Beach seines, like gill nets, had a cork line and a lead line, but their construction and operation were quite different. The webbing of big beach seines—some as long as 1,200 to 1,800 yards, always operated by teams of fisherman—consisted of coarse-meshed wings on either end of a fine-meshed pocket or bag, in which the captured fish were collected. Because seines work by entrapment, these nets were not size-selective, taking nearly everything they encircled. Typically, the wing ropes of one end of a big beach seine were secured by half of the beach crew as the other end of the net was carried offshore by a boat that passed around the school of fish before returning to shore and passing the ropes of the other wing to the other half of the beach crew. The net and fish were then dragged shoreward by main force, but the catch was not beached. Instead, the wings were transferred to boats, from which the fish trapped in the bag could be scooped (or brailed) out.[1]

R.S.V

The black or striped mullet (*Mugil cephalus*) is one of the finest eating fish in Florida and one of the least appreciated. It is caught by cast net or seine from Fernandina to the Panhandle. On the east coast and around the Ten Thousand Islands it is firm-fleshed and delicious, but along the west coast, after a few weeks feeding on the white, muddy bottom of the estuaries and lagoons, it loses its greenish black-and-silver color and becomes grayish. The flesh of west coast mullet, to my mind, has a muddy flavor.

Along the east coast and the Keys, the mullet make an annual migration, although little has been written about this in the fisheries literature or elsewhere. In the fall, when the nor'easters begin to blow, great schools of mullet appear on the north Florida coast and move slowly southward along the beaches. As they pass the various inlets, some move into the coastal lagoons on the flood tide and may be separated from the main school or rejoin it on the ebb. Slowly the school moves southward, its flanks attacked by marauding jacks, sharks, bluefish, and other predators. The school may stretch for hundreds of yards along the beach, and from the water's edge to well beyond the breakers. And this will be only one of many schools. In the Keys they pass through the islands and into the shallow waters of Florida Bay. For weeks the bay will fill with fish until the waters of Snake Bight, Madeira Bay, Dildo Bank, and Conchie Joe Channel are filled with them.

In the early days most of the mullet were caught along the open beach using huge beach seines or by purse boats. Today fishing is relegated to gill-netting in the bays and lagoons and to cast-netters. The last great beach seine haul in south Florida was made in 1940, when Cap Knight made the final set with the "Bear." Unfortunately, I was there.

In those days if you drove north from Hillsboro Inlet along Highway A1A, a short distance from the lighthouse, you would see a big sign on the opposite bank of the canal, painted in blue and yellow, proclaiming that this was "Cap's Place." There was a rickety dock on the bank and a boardwalk that led off through the mangroves to some bright blue buildings. Alongside the road were a small parking place, a landing stage, and a sign that informed you to blow your horn.

If you followed these instructions an elderly figure would untie a skiff or flattie from the far bank and leisurely row across to ferry you to the far side. If it was dark the boardwalk was illuminated by light bulbs strung from poles in the mangroves. A short walk brought you to the first building on the right. It housed a bar and a small casino with croupiers and stick men in evening clothes, incongruous in the rustic setting of blue walls and bare floors. A few feet farther on and you entered the main building, also painted blue. By now it was obvious that Cap liked blue.

This was the restaurant, and the floors were bare pine and the tables were well-scrubbed planks. Fish nets, patched and mended, were draped around the walls and hung from the ceilings, while various flotsam and jetsam decorated the walls: old wooden shoes, Japanese net floats, lobster pot buoys, and turtle shells. But the main attraction was Cap Knight himself. There might be a dress code for others, but not for Cap. He walked about barefoot and shirtless. A big, broad-shouldered, barrel-chested man, hairy and long and powerful of arm, dressed only in a pair of ragged pants and an old captain's cap, he was rough-mannered and short of temper.

The menu was small, but the food was superb. Cap's steaks were thick and juicy and done to perfection. Fresh fish, caught from his own boats, were served simply, with no degenerate sauces to obscure their true flavor. As an appetizer or entree there were turtle-egg pancakes, the eggs dug fresh on the opposite beach, and nearly everyone ordered the delicate "heart of palm" salad. The food and Cap were perfect complements to one another. And if you did not like one or the other or both, and said so, you did not come back. People packed into Cap's Place in chauffeur-driven cars from Palm Beach or Miami or arrived in seaplanes that landed on the lake behind the restaurant.

If anyone did complain about the food, an unusual event, Cap was prone to take direct action, as one of America's famous millionaires discovered one evening. Hardly had his complaint reached Cap's ears than he was caught by the back of his coat, marched down to the dock and heaved into the canal.

"And don't come back," Cap ordered, as the ferryman hauled the dripping, unwanted guest from the water.

The following night a cavalcade of cars drove up and honked their united horns. Amid a crowd of admiring friends, the millionaire met Cap, slapped him on the back and announced to his party, "Meet Cap Knight. This is the man who threw me off the end of the dock last night. I warn you, don't complain about the food, or that's where you'll end up too." The millionaire and Cap became good friends.[2]

There was little about any kind of fish that Cap did not know. He had been captain of fishing smacks and schooners, a gillnetter, a mackerel squidder, and a middle-ground fisherman. He also owned a gigantic beach seine with a pocket that could hold 150,000 pounds of fish. It was known as the Bear.

For some reason Cap decided in the fall of 1940 that he was going to set the Bear for mullet and make a killing. To be worthwhile it had to be a big school, and with 150,000 pounds of fish in the bag, the set had to be made at a place where the catch could be run to the dock and waiting trucks quickly and iced down in the fish house. Cap decided that the best place was close to his own on the beach just south of Hillsboro Inlet.

Somewhere south of Cape Canaveral a gigantic mass of mullet was sighted and reported to Cap Knight. As it moved southward reports became more numerous, until Cap finally scouted it himself north of Palm Beach. It passed Lake Worth, was barely affected by Boca Raton Inlet, and finally, on the morning of a calm day in October, it reached Hillsboro.

Cap was ready. The Bear was piled into his big sea skiff, and with his nephew Burnham in another, they went out the inlet and down the beach to where the beach crew was waiting. There were about a dozen of us, and our job was to haul the wings of the net ashore and pull the bag down.

The water was gin clear, the white bottom reflecting the rays of the early morning sun. Along the shore the black mass of the mullet stretched from the lighthouse, set among the Australian pines and seagrapes, down the beach as far as where we stood. The tide was ebbing, and the current was flowing out of Hillsboro as the mullet passed Lighthouse Point and moved across the rocky bar. They covered the sand, and there were hundreds of thousands of pounds of them, packed tightly from the surface to the bottom.

Here and there in the dark mass were a few fish swimming upside down, their white bellies in sharp contrast to the dark backs of the others. For some reason, mullet get their organs of balance (statoliths) upset, and a few are always found swimming upside down. As they stand out in stark contrast to the others, they probably don't survive very long among their many predators.

Cap Knight slowly cruised back and forth in front of the school, looking it over, and finally gave the word to start the set. The skiff with the net ran in to the beach and passed the wing ropes to the first shore party, which dug into the sand and held on as the big boat slowly ran the net out into the middle of the school, turned south, and then headed back in to the shore to pass the wing ropes of the other end to the second shore party. The school was so big that the Bear only took in a minute fraction of the whole mass, which continued down the beach as if nothing had happened, seemingly undiminished.

Both crews now put their backs into it and slowly dragged the pocket toward the beach, with Cap shouting encouragement to the crews and cursing as mullet flowed under the foot rope.

"By God, they're getting away," he roared. "Pull on that damned net."

It must have taken an hour of unmerciful, backbreaking hauling in sun that was now blazing hot to drag that big pocket into

Florida fishermen hauling on the lead line of a big beach seine; the slack cork line lies in the water to their left. Photo by J. J. Steinmetz, 1940s; State Archives of Florida.

shallow water. There were at least 150,000 pounds of mullet in it, and it would come no further, pull as we might. The wings were now piled into the two sea skiffs and pulled taut, the bag held in place, opening up, between the two boats. Everyone was elated.

"Man, have we got the fish. We're going to make a bundle out of this," we told each other over and over as we admired our catch.

By now the sun was high in the sky, and brailing out began. We soon found, however, that we couldn't move the fish fast enough. We needed two sea skiffs to carry away the fish to the waiting trucks, and we needed more trucks and ice. As the sun rose higher and higher the shallow water warmed; in that packed mass of fish it was even warmer, and all the oxygen was used up.

We had not brailed more than about 20,000 pounds when Cap started looking worried and his nose began to twitch.

"Boys," he said, "we'd better handle those fish faster. They're beginning to die and bloat."

This was all too evident. Burnham suggested that the two sea skiffs tow the bag into deeper water, farther offshore where it was cooler; but both skiffs, despite their powerful engines, could not budge the bag. Dozens of sharks had congregated and were tearing at the webbing. By now we all realized there was no hope of saving the rest of the fish; they were rotting in the net.

"Men," declared Cap (we had matured quickly), "we've got to spill those fish out of the net and turn them loose. Hook a couple of grapnels on the shore side of the bottom of the bag and let's turn the net on its side."

But no amount of pulling on the grapnels could move that great mass of fish.

"There's only one thing for it," Cap declared, "we've got to rip the bottom out of the net. Make the wings fast and open those engines full throttle, that'll do it."

But it didn't. Nothing happened, and the stench was growing.

At this Burnham slipped off his shirt and shoes, took a bait knife he had been sharpening, and slid overboard right in among the mullet and the sharks. The water was churned white on the outside of the net by the sand sharks and bull sharks ripping at the webbing and gorging on mullet. Some swam about with mullet tails sticking out of their distended jaws. Burnham dived to the bottom, right into this mess, and made a long slit in the side of the net. To my amazement he came up unscathed and unconcerned. With both engines again at full throttle, at last the fish began to spill from the bag. Then it split open, and more than 100,000 pounds of dead and dying mullet spilled out into the water.

It was now midafternoon. There was a slight westerly wind, and the tide was ebbing.

"They'll drift offshore and be gone by the time the tide changes," Cap said.

We were tired, hot, and exhausted as we got back to the dock. But we were far from finished. Many of the mullet were small. Cap took us up to the fish house and handed each of us a stick cut to the minimum length. We now had to go through all those iced fish and measure every one of them. If the fish was shorter than the stick, out it went. Measuring 20,000 pounds of fish is slow work. By the time we had finished it was long after dark, and all I wanted was a shower, something to eat, and bed.

I had hardly fallen asleep, or so it seemed, when someone was shaking me.

"Come on, get up, the fish have come ashore."

"They've what?" I asked.

"The fish have come ashore." It was Burnham speaking. "The wind changed and blew them all back onto the beach, and there are dead mullet from the lighthouse to Las Olas Boulevard in Fort Lauderdale. The health officials have been to see Cap, and if we don't bury them all there's going to be a court case and fines for all of us. Come on, everyone's in the truck with shovels."

And bury them we did. There was a black line of dead mullet about three feet wide on the beach as far as we could see. We divided into groups of four: two dug holes and two raked in the mullet and covered them. We worked all day with sunburned backs and blistered hands. Cap kept coming by with ice water, urging us on.

We passed Lauderdale by the Sea, and still those damned

mullet, smelling to high heaven but getting fewer as we worked, lay ahead of us. By the time we got to Fort Lauderdale Beach there were only a few scattered ones left, and the sea was building and washing them back offshore. When we reached the end of Las Olas Boulevard the mullet had ended, and so had we.

Burnham spoke for us all as we leaned on our shovels at the last hole. "I hope I never see or smell another damned mullet." He paused. "I think I'll burn that damned Bear too."

A week later Cap came by with the check for my share of the haul. It was $6.35. I never saw or heard of the Bear again. Maybe Burnham did burn it. I hope so.

4

The Cast-Netters

*Lake Worth was a freshwater lake when the first settlers
arrived. Fed by springs along its western shoreline, it
was diked against the sea on its eastern side by the high
dunes of the ocean ridge. Slightly higher than sea level, it
sometimes overflowed across the lowest part of the ridge
after hurricanes or exceptionally heavy summer rains;
when the torrent was spent, salt water spilled into the lake
for a few days or weeks, but these were temporary breaches
soon repaired by the surf, and the lake remained fresh.
The first more or less permanent inlet, dug by the pioneers
themselves in 1877 at the north end of the lake (not far
from the present site of Palm Beach Inlet), permanently
lowered the level of the lake and began its transformation
into the saltwater lagoon it is today. A second inlet,
excavated at the south end of the lake in 1927, helped to
complete the transformation. Known locally as Boynton
Inlet, this was to become an important center for the
sportfishing industry in the years to come.*

*The lake waters surrounding the north and south inlets
now teemed with marine species: bluefish and mackerel
in their season, pompano year-round. Sheepshead, drum,
mangrove snapper, and others swarmed around the docks.
Farther from the inlets, brackish-water species were also
abundant: lookdowns, sand perch, black mullet, silver mullet,
and snook. Oysters, introduced to the lake from Indian River,*

*also thrived and formed extensive reefs at the north and
south ends. Not without reason, Lake Worth seemed a
fisherman's dream come true in the first few decades of the
twentieth century.*[1]

R.S.V.

Cast net fishing in Florida is rapidly becoming a lost art. Cast
nets are still used, principally by bait fishermen, but those are
mostly small nets, hardly the diameter of your dining room
table, and fine-meshed. It takes about half the skill of a pizza
maker to twirl those little nets out over the water, and no self-
respecting fish would wait around for it to fall.

Gone almost to extinction are the big cast nets, 10 to 12 feet
long, with a 20-foot spread. And few net makers are around any-
more who could make one. Above all, there is hardly anyone who
could throw one, opening its full circumference to take mullet,
sand perch, lookdowns, moonfish, and even permit and pompano.

A good cast-netter, in the 1920s through the war years, could
make a living with his net catching fish for the market or bait
for the sportsfishermen. Cast-netting took little capital, because
most cast net fishermen made their own nets, and the major-
ity waded the lake. Others used a flat-bottomed skiff, poling it
along while standing in the bow with net ready to hand.

One of the best I knew was Buddy Rogers, a backwoods
cracker who cast-netted during the day and spent most of his
nights frog-leg hunting. Buddy's feet were tougher than shoe
leather, and he could wade across oyster beds barefoot with
never a care or a cut. Buddy was a market cast-netter, mainly
after black or striped mullet, at the catching of which he was
an expert. He used a nine-foot net and threw it flat across the
water, just skimming the surface, to the exact point where he
wanted it to land, or rather sink. And he had an eye for just
where the fish were. He seldom made a dry haul.

In the early days of our charterboat fishing, unless one used ballyhoo for bait, the captains and the mates caught their own bait, the preferred kind being silver or white mullet, but big blacks were also used. This meant that after coming in from a long day's fishing, I had to get my cast net and go in search of bait. A small-mesh net was used for small silver mullet hiding near the water's edge along the grass, but large ones were either caught by wading the shore or by poling a skiff in deeper water.

During the day this offered little hazard if you watched what you were doing, but at night, when the net was brought aboard, it frequently had a stingray in it, and the chances of getting a spine in your leg or thigh were rather high. If the spine broke off, there were often difficulties getting it out, because the edges of the spine are equipped with a row of teeth. A spining would often cause a short spell of nausea and faintness. The usual cure for getting spined was to open the wound as far as possible and pour kerosene into it. Most cast-netters kept a bottle of kerosene in their skiff for this purpose.

A good cast net in those days was handmade of linen net twine using a net needle and a mesh board. The horn end of the net was made of 36 meshes across, and was straight for about a foot, after which length a widener was put in every two meshes on every third row. This made the net, when the two edges were sewn together, form a little more than a full circle when laid out flat. On a good net, the last foot had no wideners so that it formed a wall, the idea being that the wall would sink straight down and keep fish from escaping under the net. When the net was finished, a lead line with cast net sinkers was fastened to the edge, and eighteen tuck lines were tied to the lead line at the position of each of the rows of wideners, the other ends being tied to the handline by which it was pulled. The top of the net was securely fastened around a metal thimble or one made of bone or horn.

This is quite a different net than the ones shown in travel advertisements with a South Sea islander throwing his net. His net has no tuck lines and no line to retrieve it. To get his fish he has to swim around it, slowly working the lead line in by hand until the net is bunched up and the fish can be carried ashore.

To throw a net was simple. One straightened out the net so that the tuck lines were straight and the webbing extended to its full length. About one third of the net was held in the right hand, about four feet from the lead line, and the rest was held in the left hand. The slack section between the two hands was held lightly between the teeth. The net was thrown with a half turn of the body and a swing of the arms out over the water and level with the surface. As it was thrown, you let go of the line in your mouth. Properly thrown, the net sailed out just a few feet above the water, spread out in a circle, and dropped cleanly into the water. If you were wearing dentures and forgot to let go quickly enough, the dentures also swept out over the water, as has happened on more than one occasion to unfortunate cast-netters.

When the net settled to the bottom, one could usually tell if the cast was successful by the tugging on the line as fish hit the webbing. A few quick jerks on the handline would bring the tuck lines together, tucking the lead line in, and holding the fish in the bag of the net. Lifting the horn and pulling the net straight and lifting it off the sand or bottom of the boat would let the fish out. A flip of the lead line would clear the net, and you were ready for another cast. But it was an art, and I have known people who never mastered it, the net landing in the water in a clump of leads, scaring every fish within hearing distance.

Lake Worth was a cast-netter's paradise. Big eating mullet (this was in the days when the lake was not polluted) could be caught from the bridges and docks. Using a large-mesh net, a single cast in the lagoon between Hypoluxo Island and the beach ridge in Lantana could always be depended upon to capture enough lookdowns—beautiful, flat, silvery fish with roman noses—or a net full of sand perch for dinner. At Boynton Inlet, silversides came in so thick that a single cast would catch a bucketful. And at night shrimp could be caught with a bait net.

If you did not own a cast net, it was usually because you had never learned to throw one, could not afford the price for anything larger than a bait net, or did not have the patience to make one yourself. A small-mesh bait net was never very long because it took too much time to make. On the other hand, a large-mesh net for sand perch or lookdowns could be made in a few hours, if one was a fast worker. Later, machine-made nets appeared, but they were never as good as hand-made nets.

Today little cast-netting is seen in east and south Florida, but it is still practiced in the shallow bays and estuaries along the Gulf Coast. Most people are unaware of cast-netting, except for those picturesque ads showing a Polynesian fisherman flinging a cast net high into the air against the rays of the setting sun. In Florida he would starve to death.

5

Snapper Fishermen

Red snapper, a strikingly handsome species long prized by diners, have been fished commercially in the Gulf of Mexico since before the Civil War. The earliest Gulf snapper fishery consisted of New England schooners and crews based at Pensacola; this fleet mostly fished inside the 50-fathom line from Mobile, Alabama, to Fort Walton, Florida, and most of the catch was marketed at New Orleans. At first snapper were brought to port in live wells, but this limited the fleet to nearshore fishing because snapper could only be maintained alive for a few days. Live wells fell out of favor when inexpensive manufactured ice became available in the mid-1890s. Schooners with stored ice could fish much farther from shore, and iced fish could be transported hundreds of miles inland by rail, resulting in a much larger market for the catch.

By the mid-1930s the Gulf snapper fleet consisted of large schooners, most with auxiliary gasoline engines, based at Galveston, Mobile, Pensacola, and Tampa; these fleets mostly fished the Campeche Bank off the Yucatán Peninsula. The fleets out of Panama City, Carrabelle, and other small ports, however, used smaller vessels and mostly fished in national waters, including the so-called Middle Ground reef complex on the Florida Shelf.

Because productive snapper grounds are in deep water over irregular rocky bottom, this was traditionally a

*handline fishery. Handlines were made of no. 12 tarred
cotton line about 100 fathoms in length, each rigged with
a lead weight and two to three baited hooks. The smaller
schooners, such as those based out of Carrabelle, were
typically crewed by four to five fishermen, held only 8 to 10
tons of ice, and spent a maximum of ten days or so at sea.[1]*

R.S.V.

It was blowing a howling sou'easter when we came through
Carrabelle Pass. We had just made the run from New Orleans
when the blow began, and the seas were building hourly. It was
no place for even an 85-foot houseboat of the old yacht type,
and we were glad to get in out of the seas. As we made our way
in Johnny DeLettre, the captain, swept the waterfront with
his binoculars. The snapper fleet had raced in from the Middle
Ground with the first onslaught of the blow, and the harbor was
a maze of masts.

The small, high-sided, two-masted schooners, weatherbeaten
and dumpy, filled almost all the dock space in the harbor. The
crews were still furling and lashing down the sails, and hatches
were being opened. Big wire baskets filled with red snapper were
being hoisted from the holds and dumped into wooden carts
that were trundled up the wharves to the fish houses. Other
schooners were being washed down.

After finding a berth and securing, Johnny and I walked over
to the nearest fish house, where another schooner had just come
in. Standing out of the way we watched as the crew, using long
steel hooks, pulled the fish out of the ice in the hold and slung
them into waiting baskets. The fish were silver-bellied and red or
pink on the sides and back. There were a few big grouper.

The fishermen were dressed nondescriptly, crackers, lean,
gaunt, and grizzled. Bottles were being passed back and forth
among the crew, and voices were rising. In another hour they'd

napper smack from Carrabelle. Small schooners like these usually fished the Florida
iddle Ground rather than the Campeche Bank. Photographer unknown, after 1925;
ate Archives of Florida.

be in the bars getting up a full head of steam before heading for home. Girls were beginning to drift down to the wharves, and wives were trying to get husbands home before they got too liquored up.

It was a typical scene going on in all the snapper ports from Biloxi to Pensacola, Port St. Joe to Tampa. In a week they would all be broke and waiting for the wind to lay, so they could get back to the Middle Ground or the Campeche Bank.

The snapper boat crews of the Panhandle were not traditional fishermen. Many had wandered down from the cow towns or from Georgia.[2] They drank their money away and took little pride in their profession or in their schooners. Many years later I was at a meeting on fisheries problems in the Gulf of Mexico. One of the speakers recommended that the entire snapper-boat fishing fraternity should be fired and replaced with Italian or Spanish fishermen with a tradition of the sea.

The next morning it was blowing a full gale. When it was over, ten days later, we knew Carrabelle from one end to the other. It was a wild frontier town, and perhaps the only one wilder was its neighbor, Wewahitchka. Both were cow towns as well, and it was hard to say which group—fishermen or cowboys—was the wilder.

With my week's wages I went up to the local barbershop for a shave and a haircut. The barber had finished cutting my hair and was beginning to lather my neck and face when a man came in.

"Well, Joe, ain't seen you fer some time. Thought you'd moved to Wewahitchka?"

"I did," the barber replied, stropping his razor. He tilted my head back. "Had to leave."

"What fer?"

"Oh, some damned furriner from Georgia came in and asked for a shave. He got to arguin,' then cursin,' called my old woman a whore, and I slit his throat." He drew the razor up and over my Adam's apple, which was bobbing as I swallowed, heart in my mouth. "Hold still," he commanded, "or you're liable to get nicked."

He turned back to his friend as he wiped the lather off his blade. "He bled something terrible, really messed up the shop."

He paused. "Sheriff said it was self-defense but told me I'd better get out of town for a while. I'll go back when it blows over."

I never moved a muscle until he finished. I gave him a generous tip and left. He was still discussing the gory details as I walked out of his shop.

There was a football game between the two high schools while we were stormbound, and we went to see it. The field was mowed stubble, and there were no bleachers. The teams came onto the field in uniform, and the punter kicked the ball barefoot. The rest of the spectators were on cow ponies. As the ball was caught at the opposite end of the field, the whole crowd galloped to the other end, and we barely missed being trampled to death. Back and forth went the ball, back and forth went the cow ponies, their riders whooping and yelling. We dodged and sidestepped and finally retreated to watch the game from behind a wall of horses' legs and cowboy boots. I don't recall whether Carrabelle or Wewahitchka won or what the score was.

"Carrabelle just warn't no safe place for a furriner, no how."

6

~~~~~~~~

Tight Lines!

The Gulf Stream hugs the coastline of southeast Florida. It is so close that from the crest of the dunes near Boynton you can see it on the horizon, a broad stretch of deep blue beyond the bright green inshore water. Only a few miles away, its tropical influence is felt right up onto the beach. The proximity of Palm Beach County's shoreline to the great current accounts for much of the distinctive marine ecology of the region and for its enduring popularity among sportsfishermen.

Florida's marine sportfishing industry, worth billions of dollars annually by the end of the twentieth century, had its modest beginnings in the 1920s and early 1930s at small marinas scattered along the east coast, mostly between Stuart and Miami. Some of the species fished for sport, like kingfish, had previously been taken commercially, but others were virtually unknown to local fishermen before gamefishing caught on. One of these was the Atlantic sailfish.

Large and spectacular fighters prized by anglers for their fast runs, high leaps, and tailwalking when hooked, sailfish are not particularly good to eat, and they were probably regarded as a nuisance by the commercial fishermen, who sometimes caught them on handlines while kingfishing. A few bold anglers, intrigued by descriptions of these hard-fighting fish—immediately recognizable by

*their swordlike bill, high purplish sail, and deeply forked
tail—began handlining for them on purpose. But the sport
did not take off until the art of playing them with rod and
reel was developed.*

*Almost nothing was known about the biology of sailfish
when the Voss brothers began fishing for them in the late
1930s. The observations Gil made in 1940 would later
be summarized as part of a scientific report, the first
substantial contribution to the natural history of the
species. Even today, many aspects of the life history of
these large and beautiful fish remain unknown.*[1]

R.S.V.

It was a beautiful clear day with a few fluffy white clouds and
a calm sea as we passed over the bar at Stuart Inlet. Our party
of anglers was below in the cockpit applying sunburn lotion.
Walter and I were on the flying bridge of the DREAM GIRL, a
36-foot Backus cabin sea skiff, running offshore to where, in the
distance, we could see scattered flocks of sea birds, mainly pelicans, wheeling and diving with their usual cumbersome splash.

Several other boats were out, each heading for its own flock
of birds. Walter picked out one and headed the DREAM GIRL for
it. I dropped down into the cockpit and went aft.

"We're coming onto the fish now," I announced. "Who is first?
Only one person can fish at a time."

"No outriggers?" Mr. Sarazin asked.

"Not on these fish. This is completely different fishing than
you've ever done before for sailfish. Here, we are on the fish now."

Walter slowed the boat about a hundred feet from the
screaming, diving birds, turned her around, and slowly backed
down toward the melee.

Mr. Sarazin turned, saw what was happening, and grabbed
his movie camera. "My God, I've never seen anything like this."

Just astern of the DREAM GIRL was a school of small fish, pilchards, being herded into a tight mass by about fifteen or twenty sailfish circling around them, their sails half out of water. Seagulls were diving into the pilchards and fighting one another for their prey. Among them circled and wheeled big brown pelicans, which were diving at the sails of the sailfish. Just then a big pelican dived at one near our stern, grabbed the sail in its bill, and tried to lift it out of the water. The sailfish broke free and continued its circling of the pilchards.

"What are the sailfish doing?" Mr. Sarazin asked, pausing in his filming.

"Just watch. They're keeping the pilchards herded up tight so that they can catch them more easily. There goes one now." I pointed to a sailfish that had turned away from its fellows. It circled away, swam down below the others, and slowly swam through the pilchards, slashing right and left with its long, bony bill.

Stunned and dying pilchards sank downward, and the sailfish turned and leisurely ate them one after the other. When it had finished off its kill, it returned to the surface and began circling again. The movie camera hummed, taking it all in.

I took one of the silver mullet from the bait box and rigged it on one of the lines. It was a small silver, not much larger than one of the pilchards, cast-netted by me the evening before in the St. Lucie River. Sarazin took up a rod and stood by while I stripped off about 20 feet of line, coiling it carefully on the stern. I waited until another sailfish dropped down to go through the pilchards. As it did, I threw the bait into the water, letting out the line so that it sank down among the stunned pilchards. The big fish turned, gobbled up the pilchards, and took the mullet too. As the line came tight, Sarazin set the hook.

Instantly the sailfish took off, the reel screaming. Sarazin was an experienced angler and fought the sail standing up, the rod butt in a belt harness. The sailfish surfaced, gave a spectacular

Walter's first DREAM GIRL, a 36-foot Backus cabin sea skiff. A flying bridge was added sometime around 1940. Later boats, designed and outfitted by Walter and also called DREAM GIRL, would become legendary among sports-fishermen around the world. Photographer unknown, ca. 1939.

jump, dived, and then tailwalked half way around the DREAM GIRL, Walter turning to keep the fish over the stern. Again and again the fish jumped, slatting its head from side to side, trying to throw the hook. The bait sailed through the air, but the hook held, and slowly Sarazin brought the tiring fish to the side.

"Let it go to fight again," he said.

I picked up my pliers, took hold of the leader, slid the pliers down the wire until they were against the fish's jaw, and snipped the wire. The sail lay nearly still for a moment or two, slowly began to swim away, and then returned to the feeding frenzy with its mates. On the flying bridge Walter tied a white flag onto the outrigger halyard and hoisted it up toward the top. It was the first of eighteen release flags that went up that day.

We backed down into the milling fish again, and I rigged up for another angler. A seagull dived at the bait, trying to take it away from me. Sailfish rubbed up against the boat. One of the party reached over the side and seized a dorsal fin, only to have it slide through his fingers. One sail bumped the stern of the boat with its bill, breaking off a half inch of it in the soft white-cedar planking. We hooked another fish.

One of the fish was fought almost to the side of the boat, but just before I could reach out for the leader, it pulled free. The angler looked up to see if a release flag was added to the string decorating the port outrigger. I shook my head.

"The only release is when I've taken hold of the leader and have the fish under my control. I can then either pull the leader free, pull out the hook, or cut the fish free. Then it's a release."

"Do all of these released fish live with hooks in their jaws? I should think it would be better to bring the fish on board and remove the hook with pliers."

"No, that hurts the fish more than leaving the hook in. We often catch a sailfish with five or six hook scars in its mouth, usually stained with rust. The sea water corrodes the hook away quickly. We only bring the fish aboard if it's hooked deep and obviously hurt. Then an ice pick in its brain kills it instantly."

Sail after sail was hooked, jumped, and was released. I cut the barb off Sarazin's hook. The sail would jump once or twice, throw the hook, and swim back to its fellows. Sarazin and his party were sportsmen, not killers, and needed no pictures of dead fish hung on the fish racks at the dock. Nor did we need fish as advertisement; our release flags told the story.

As the day wore on, the school of pilchards became smaller and smaller as the sails consumed them. By early afternoon they were gone, and so were the sailfish and the birds. Next morning other pilchards would be rounded up, and the same fishing would go on. This daily concentration of sailfish in the waters off Stuart had gone on for several weeks now and brought boats from as far away as Palm Beach to fish the schools. It was undoubtedly the concentrations of pilchards that attracted the sailfish, and it was to continue like this for several more days. Every afternoon the sailfish scattered after the pilchard schools were devoured, and the boats then returned to regular trolling for sails and other fish. Often, however, the rest of the day was more relaxation than real fishing.

But that particular evening a nor'wester began to blow, and by the second day the ground swells on Gilbert's Bar, the entrance to the St. Lucie, had become dangerously high for the uninitiated. That morning, when we went out, a lifeboat from the Gilbert's Bar Coast Guard station was down inside the bar warning boatmen that the bar was dangerous and that the boats should not go out.

Walter and I looked it over from the flying bridge. The combers breaking on the bar were 10 to 15 feet high, but as usual with a nor'wester, the sea outside was calm, and we knew that the fishing would be good. Several of the local boats were already out. We were used to such seas on the bar at Boynton, so we closed the forward hatch and asked the party of anglers—again Mr. Sarazin and friends—to sit down and be careful. We waited our time just inside the break, and when there was a lull between the big seas, we opened the throttle and ran over the bar. A small sea built up just outside, Walter slowed to take it easily, and then we were clear. But we knew the seas would be larger and more dangerous in the evening.

We had an excellent day of fishing: sailfish, dolphin, a few little tunies. Although cold, the day was beautiful, with only a small chop. At about five o'clock we were off the inlet along with a small gathering of other boats. From seaward, looking at the back side of the rollers, the inlet did not look too bad, but the seas by now were running at least 18 feet high on the bar. Jack Whitaker, the only local captain with experience on the bar, was lying outside the break watching for a calm period to go in. It is an unwritten but well-understood rule that the first boat in has the right of way for running an inlet, and that no one else attempts it unless the first boat waves another on. Behind us were two new boats from Salerno, both with New Jersey captains, 38-foot Matthews cruisers rigged as sportsfishermen.

Jack finally saw the break in the ground swells that he wanted, poured on the power, and went over the bar into the smooth water inside. He took his boat over to the front range for the bar and turned around to wait for the next boat. The ranges marking the channel were fine all day except in the evening, when they lay directly in front of the setting sun and were hard to see. It was customary for each boat to lay on the range so that the next boat could see the channel.

It was now our turn. From just outside the bar the seas looked enormous. I closed the hatch leading down below and had the party put on life jackets and sit down. Then I took out the big steel tiller and fitted it on. If the DREAM GIRL was to broach or start to, I could put more strain onto the rudder from the tiller than Walter could from the wheel on the flying bridge. From down below I could judge the size of the seas astern of us better than Walter on the flying bridge, but he could tell whether there was a break showing up the beach.

Finally Walter called that there was a break and eased the throttle up. I looked astern; there was only a small grounder making up, and I called to Walter. He waited until it was just under our stern and opened the engine wide open. The sea rode up under us, caught us about amidships, and we flew over the bar on the crest like a surf board. We were just about on top of the bar when I yelled to Walter: one of the Matthews cruisers was trying to run the bar on our sea but had not caught the sea and was starting to fall off ahead of it. The bow dropped and caught in the water, luckily at an angle away from us, the stern was carried forward by the sea, and she went into a broach, turned broadside, and rolled over, filling with water. If she had broached in the other direction she would have cut us in two.

Captain, mate, and four fishermen were in the water. Jack had seen what was happening and was already running down to them while we were still on the wave crest. He picked up the people in the water and came back in, leaving the boat to drift into the river. We ran over to the range and turned around for the next boat. I had my qualms about it.

"Quick, get your camera," I told Mr. Sarazin. "Just focus on the white spot of the boat that is coming in, and when I say 'shoot,' start it rolling." He nodded.

The next boat did not wait properly for a break in the seas and caught a big one. Nearly to the bar the bow dropped and I told Sarazin to press the button and hold it down. In a moment the bow dropped into the trough, the forefoot caught on the rock reef, and the big 38-footer tripped and pitchpoled, flipping end over end. Sarazin kept the movie camera going through the whole thing and continued to shoot as we ran down to the boat and pulled the people out of the water. In less than ten minutes two boats belonging to the same person were lost on the bar from ignorance.

Later, when the film was developed, Mr. Sarazin asked us up to the hotel for the first showing. It was spectacular, probably the first movie of the loss of a boat in the surf.

With the winter fishing season of 1940–41 over, we brought the DREAM GIRL back to Boynton and Walter turned her over to me while he went to Beach Haven, New Jersey, for the summer. At that time no one thought that there were any fish in Florida during the summer, and almost all the boats went north, as we had done before, to Ocean City, Maryland, to fish white marlin. But I was certain that there was as good summer fishing in Florida,

Fish Haven Charter Boat Captains Swap Fish Stories

FISH HAVEN ANGLERS' CLUB

HAROLD LYMAN OF THE "WEEZIE"

FRED VOSS OF THE "LUCKY LADY"

MRS. C.C. COOK OF THE "ADA."

HERBIE SCHMIDZ OF THE "DOROTHY"

C.C. COOK OF FISH HAVEN

KENNETH LYMAN OF THE "WEEZIE"

GIL VOSS OF THE "DREAM GIRL"

WALTER VOSS OF THE "DREAM GIRL"

GYP THE FISH HOUND

MATT RICHEY OF THE "LUCKY LADY"

JACK WILLIAMS OF THE "DOROTHY"

WALTER LYMAN OF THE "IRIS"

BUD COOK OF THE "ADA"

Herb Roth.

Cartoon by Herb Roth that appeared in the *Delray Beach News* on February 21, 1941. "Fish Haven" was the local name for the charterboat docks on the west side of Lake Worth just opposite Boynton Inlet.

perhaps even better, if one only worked at it. I wrote to one of our real sporting fishermen and his wife, suggesting that they come down for a week of fishing at bargain prices and they took me up on it.

Never had fishing been so good. We would leave the dock before eight o'clock and run out to the weed line at the edge of the Gulf Stream, outrigger baits dancing at the surface. Suddenly there would be a flash of color as a wahoo came up from underneath, seized the bait, and made a spectacular leap into the air. When the line came tight after falling from the outrigger, the wahoo would make several long, vicious runs, the reel screaming, but would quickly tire and be brought to gaff and into the fish box. Occasionally we would catch a kingfish. Dolphin (dorados) lurked around the sargasso-weed line, big square-headed bulls and smaller sloping-headed females. One or two would go into the fish box, but the others were released. The early forenoon was also the best for trolling for sailfish along the weed line, but one morning I tried something else.

Coming out of the inlet I turned north just off the beach and seaward of the shallow inner reef, which in places was nearly bare at low tide but often had five or six feet of water on it. I ran along with the port outrigger skipping along almost on top of the reef when suddenly there was a tremendous burst of spray, the outrigger line dropped out, and the line came tight. It was as if we were anchored to the bottom. From the flying bridge I finally saw that it was a big grouper that had taken the outrigger bait. At the side my mate cut it free and re-rigged the line.

A few hundred yards farther, in no more than 10 feet of water, a sailfish rose, its bill out of water as it tried to grab the mullet. At the next strike the line snapped out of the outrigger clothespin and fell free, the sail took the bait, and the angler struck it hard. Almost immediately the sail jumped. Because of the shoal water, it fought more in the air than underwater. It was spectacular. In the shallow water with white-sand bottom, every move the fish made was visible from the flying bridge. But it was a short fight, and the fish was soon brought alongside for release. It was then that I could see how distended the stomach region was. She was a female and almost bursting with eggs.

We rigged up again, and I suggested that the angler come up on the flying bridge to fish so that the fighting fish would be visible. A few minutes later we raised another sailfish, which also turned out to be a ripe female. We raised and released four fish along the inner reef that morning as well as several more large grouper that were not kept.

The Graysons were delighted. When the trip was over I rigged a temporary fighting chair in the center of the flying bridge so that in calm weather, and especially close to the beach, the angler could see all the action that was taking place. Tommy, my mate, and I also filed the barbs off several hooks.

The next day the pattern was continued, but this time, after getting a jump or two out of each fish, the barbless hook was thrown, and the fish escaped. We could not run up a release flag, but everyone was pleased, including the fish. Fortunately the Graysons were real anglers, enjoying the thrill of the strike and the jump, not of killing the fish.

Afternoons were often spent on one of the amberjack holes fishing with live bait, usually a goggle-eye or a blue runner. The fish was hooked lightly near the tail, so that it had to swim downward and free-spooled until it reached the bottom. Action was always fast as an amberjack, grouper, or African pompano would inhale the bait and a stiff fight was waged between angler and fish.

Big amberjack were few in the summer, but small ones were often taken. The prize was always an African pompano: big, thin, high, silvery fish with long dorsal and ventral fins. They were so flat that each shake of the head was like putting on the brakes. Beautiful fish, in the Palm Beach area they are never common. All were released. We also trolled the weed line in the afternoons, and if a large dolphin was caught it was kept to be cooked for dinner at the inlet restaurant.

Neither of the other two captains who were summer fishing from the inlet believed us about the sailfish and where we were raising them. Indeed, without release flags, they did not believe that we were seeing sailfish along the shore at all, until one day a sailfish tailwalked almost onto the sand, scaring some swimmers out of the water and causing a traffic jam on the beach road until it threw the hook.

It was a great two weeks for the Graysons, and they vowed to return the following summer, but international events intervened.

In the fall, with the first nor'wester, the sailfish are always found on the surface tailing—running down the big waves in the Gulf Stream with the upper lobes of their tails out of water, like a "picket fence," as the fishermen said. In the long rollers the trick was to bring the baits past and in front of the tailing fish, hoping that one would take the bait. Often both outrigger lines were taken, with a resulting double-header, or possibly all four lines. This would show not only the skill of the anglers but that of the captain trying to keep the boat in position so that lines were free. Often fish crossed over; then the rods had to be passed over or under others. It was exciting work.

Inshore, the kingfish schools were down, feeding on the shrimp coming out of the various inlets. Small kingfish were to be had for the taking, but big kings 40 pounds and upward were another matter. These were taken in our area by cutting a big black mullet in two along the backbone. Each half was rigged on two chain hooks, the hooks put in right along the edge of the back. Properly done, if the bait was towed slowly, it did not spin. Fished deep, it was irresistible to big kingfish, and 40- to 60-pounders were not unusual.

Amberjacks were now plentiful in their holes along the 85-foot reef, some weighing in at 70 and 80 pounds. Sometimes it was hard to get them away from giant barracuda that could cut the head off a 60-pound amberjack with one slash of its razor-sharp teeth.

It was in the fall that, on one trip, a commander in Naval Intelligence was among the party. He was just back from Shanghai, where he had been observing the Japanese. "Yes, war is coming," he told the others, "but it won't last long. Most of the Japanese officers and men wear glasses and have poor eyesight. I saw a vessel under cross-fire from two Japanese gunboats for forty-five minutes and not a shell hit it. They are poor marksmen."

A few days later the Japanese attacked Pearl Harbor.

Along with many other charterboatmen I enlisted in the Coast Guard. Three years later the ship I was on was nearly destroyed by one of those nearsighted Japanese pilots flying a two-engine Betty. Repaired and awaiting the expected invasion of Japan, we were in Leyte Bay when I received a letter from my brother saying that he had a good offer for the DREAM GIRL. Should he sell her or hold her until I got back?

"Sell her," I wrote. "The war out here looks like it will go on at least another year."

Two days later the bomb was dropped.

7

~~~~~~~~~~~~~~~~~~~~~~

The Crooked Greeks

Gil enlisted in the U.S. Coast Guard on December 22, 1941. Florida has more than 1,200 miles of coastline, so there was plenty for the wartime Coast Guard to do in the Sunshine State. German submarines began to sink oil tankers and merchant vessels along the east coast within weeks after war was declared, and they continued to do so for many months because, incredibly, shipping was not convoyed or escorted, and coastal cities were not blacked out. All the U-boats had to do was lie off Miami or Fort Lauderdale at night and wait for victims. Silhouetted against the urban glow, unescorted ships made easy targets. The death toll mounted, and Florida beaches were soon awash in crude oil from torpedoed tankers.

Infiltrators and saboteurs were another concern. Federal authorities were obsessed with the idea that spies were being landed on deserted beaches by German submarines or were being smuggled into ports aboard fishing vessels. For the former there was some evidence. (Early in the war a cache of explosives and cash was discovered buried in dune vegetation near Jacksonville, part of a thwarted Abwehr plot to sow terror and to sabotage American industry.) Urban myth of the time also had it that U-boat crews were coming ashore at night to purchase groceries and other supplies, even to take in movies at seaside theatres.

Whether or not such rumors were true, they fanned paranoia about coastal security.[1]

Because the peacetime Coast Guard did not have enough patrol boats to carry out its greatly expanded wartime responsibilities, all manner of civilian small craft were purchased and converted for inshore operations, and small bases were established in local fishing communities up and down the east and west coasts. Culture shock resulted when enlisted men from big northern cities encountered backwoods Florida communities, but even Floridian coastguardsmen were surprised by the diversity of fisherfolk they were sent to supervise and protect.

Rated as Seaman First Class, Gil was first assigned to harbor duty at Miami, where among other incidents he saw the Mexican oil tanker POTRERO DEL LLANO torpedoed on May 14, 1942, by U-564 (Reinhard Suhren commanding), with the loss of thirteen lives. Other east coast assignments followed, but on October 1 he was promoted to Boatswain's Mate First Class, and soon afterward he was given his first command, the CG 41009. She was a converted Greek sponge-diving boat, and appropriately, she was to patrol off Tarpon Springs, the home port of the Greek sponge fishery on the Gulf Coast.

Sponging was once a major industry in Florida. The Florida sponging grounds consisted of two principal regions. One (the Keys fishery) extended from Biscayne Bay to Key West, and the other (the Bay fishery) extended discontinuously along the Gulf Coast from the Anclote Keys off Tarpon Springs to Apalachee Bay. Key West was the center of the early Florida sponge industry until the late 1890s, when the fleet removed to Tarpon Springs to avoid harassment by Spanish warships during the Spanish-American conflict.

The early Florida sponge fishery was manned by black Bahamians, who hooked for sponges in shallow water, but by 1900 most of the shallow-water sponge beds were exhausted. So-called hard-hat diving for sponges in deeper water, using equipment and methods developed in the Aegean fishery of the Dodecanese, was introduced at Tarpon Springs in 1905, and its immediate commercial success led to mass immigration of Greek sponge divers and their families over the next several decades.[2]

R.S.V.

"CG," Bill Moutsatsos remarked, looking down at the Coast Guard patrol boats with the big CG and their numbers painted on their bows. "They ought to feel right at home here, CG, crooked Greeks."

Bill and I were sitting in a *taverna* on Athens Street having an afternoon cup of Turkish coffee. "You know, all us Greeks are crooked one way or another. The financiers are crooked and keep their divers and crews in debt by cheating them on their supply bills, the captains are crooked, trying to beat the financiers at their own game, the hookers and divers smuggle illegal sponges, and the Sponge Exchange cheats the buyers and sellers. It's our way of life," he added philosophically. "Remember, 'beware of Greeks bearing gifts.'"

"And who do you cheat?"

Bill was a baker and made most of the ship's bread used on the diving boats. He was one of the first friends I made in Tarpon Springs when I arrived with my patrol boat, the CG 41009. He was a stalwart of the Greek Orthodox Church and as honest as they come. He laughed, got up, and paid his bill.

"I haven't found a way yet, but I will."

I had just arrived in Tarpon Springs with the converted sponger, the ATHANASON. With her high bow and stern and deep draft, she was the sister ship to the dozens of brightly painted *kaikis* moored bow to the street in front of the Sponge Exchange. Instead of the gaily painted wooden rails, she had stout bulwarks, and instead of the large foremast and little jigger on the taffrail, she had a single stout mast, solid ratlines running up the shrouds to the crow's nest, and a yardarm for signal flag display.

She also mounted a .50-caliber water-cooled machine gun forward and a .30-caliber Browning on a stand atop the after cabin. She had a wheelhouse that gave her the appearance of a tugboat and also had a chart table and two bunks aft. The crew bunked below decks. She was powered with a 100-horsepower Atlas full diesel, an antique that drove my motor machinist mate quietly mad trying to keep it running. But we were the flagship of the fleet at Tarpon Springs Coast Guard base, and our duty was to lie offshore and keep watch for submarines and boats running in aliens. On our stern were four depth charges or "ash cans" equipped with delayed pressure caps that, hopefully, would allow us time to get far enough away to only get our stern blown off if we ever had to use them.[3]

Tarpon Springs was in the midst of a sponge boom, and the sponge fleet was operating at top capacity as the sponges were needed in the war effort. When we pulled into our berth at the base, the odor of drying and rotting sponges assailed my nostrils; it was an odor I was to become accustomed to smelling day and night for the next year and a half.

Sponges were everywhere; they hung in long, golden brown festoons from the rigging of the diving boats, they were heaped on the wharf along Dodecanesi Avenue, piled on the open concrete floor of the Sponge Exchange, or stored under lock and key in the exchange's vaults. This was Sponge Town, U.S.A., and the Greek divers reigned supreme. Most of the young men were now

The Greek sponge fleet at the dock in Tarpon Springs. Photographer unknown, 1946; State Archives of Florida.

in the navy, diving in heated suits with telephones, and with other new equipment their fathers had never dreamed of. The wartime divers in Tarpon Springs were therefore older, in their late thirties, forties, and fifties; dark, weather-beaten men, the sea showing from every sun-creased wrinkle. They worked on their suits or overhauled air hoses, stood in groups gesticulating and arguing in their harsh island Greek, or sat in the *tavernas* and coffee shops on Athens Street drinking *ouzo* and *masticha*, smoking cigars in their ever-present amber cigar holders, and playing their fast, table-slapping card games with fantastic stakes. I was fascinated.

We were sent out on harbor entrance duty for a couple of days to acquaint us with the sponge fleet. The guard boat lay at the mouth of the Anclote River. Each boat that went out or came in had to pass by our guard boat and give the name of the boat, name of the captain, how many gallons of fuel oil were on board, the expected area of sponging, and the number of days' supplies of provisions laid in.

We anchored at the guard site and sat back to await customers. In a few minutes one of the big new diving boats or *mekanikos* came out, and we waved her down. I jumped aboard and went aft to where the boat's crew was standing, including two Tarpon Springs blacks.

"Good morning, captain," I greeted them, readying pad and pencil. "What's the name of your boat?"

Everyone looked at me blankly. Slowly I repeated it. No answer.

"What is the name of your boat?" I repeated more loudly.

The captain waved his hands. "No spik English."

I turned to one of the blacks. "You're American. What is the name of your captain?"

The black man looked puzzled, spoke volubly in Greek to the captain, and shook his head. "No spik English. Me Greek."

Greek blacks, for God's sake.

"Doesn't anyone here speak English?" I demanded. They all looked blank. Another diving boat was coming out, and upriver I could see the masts of more.

I waved them off to one side and jumped aboard the next boat, where I got the same routine; meanwhile, the first boat started up and headed for the Gulf. I got on the radio to the base and told the commanding officer the problem.

"I know damned well they speak English and that they are just having me on," I told him. "If you'll send a relief boat out I would like twenty-four hours at the dock. Then you can send me back out tomorrow."

Back at our berth I got notebook and pencil and headed for a coffee shop on Athens Street. It was run by Georgi Paraskevas. I bought a bottle of ouzo, got two glasses, and asked George to join me. I told him what had happened.

"Now," I asked him, "how do you say 'What is the name of your boat' in Greek?"

"You'll never learn it, Voss," he told me. "There aren't but two coastguardsmen here who have learned so much as a sentence of Greek."

"You've just met the third," I told him. "I used to know a smattering of New Testament Greek. I've forgotten the alphabet, but I can transcribe in English. O.K., what is the name of your boat?"

"Ti enai to onoma tu kaikiusu?"

I wrote it down.

"What is the name of your captain?"

"Ti enai to onoma tu kapitanisu?"

"How much oil do you have?"

"Poson ladi exete?"

And so it went; more questions, the possible answers, more *ouzo*, and pronunciation drill. Other Greeks drifted in, got interested in what I was doing, and chimed in with answers.

George angrily rejected some words. "That isn't Greek, that's Italian," he would say, or Turkish. "He's going to learn Greek."

The Dodecanesi Greek of the Twelve Islands fishermen was close to the lingua franca of the Mediterranean and was filled with foreign words.

When George got busy I went over to the restaurant of his brother-in-law, Louis Pappas, and had lunch in the old building facing the waterfront and the sponge fleet. Then back for more training and cups of the thick, sweet Turkish coffee.

The next morning as we rounded to at the anchorage to relieve the other boat, it was blowing fresh from the northwest, and the Gulf was filled with whitecaps. In an hour or two we began to see boats coming back in from sea. The first looked familiar. It was my first encounter of the day before. She rounded up under our stern and I jumped aboard and walked aft.

"Ti enai to onoma tu kaikiusu?"

They all looked startled.

"Ti enai to onoma tu kapitanisu?"

Suddenly the whole crew burst out laughing and started slapping my shoulder.

"Oh, ho, so you speak Greek, eh," the captain laughed. "You sure fooled us when we came out. How you learn to speak Greek?"

I told them, and that ended it. The word spread through the fleet, and many of the captains and divers became good friends of mine. They put pressure on the captain-of-the-port to bring me in for weddings at the Greek Orthodox Church and for dinners at the Greek Hall. I was invited aboard their boats when we lay on Big Bank or rode out a blow in Cedar Key. And I drank retsina and ouzo and sang the song popular on jukeboxes at the time, "Giati, Giati?"—Why, Why?

Sponge diving is a dangerous business. The suits used at Tarpon Springs had been worn for years and had patches vulcanized at the local filling station. The brass helmets were dented and the face glasses scratched.

I first watched a sponge diver go overboard offshore of St. Martin's Reef or Big Bank. It was calm and the water clear. I lay off to starboard at a safe distance as the engineer, who usually handled the throttle and tiller, took a long steel rod with a wire basket on the end and leaned over the stern. It was a *kloubi*, a cage or propeller guard. With one on each side, if properly installed, they kept the air hose out of the propeller blades.

The diver sat forward by the diving ladder, clad in his Turkish-style seagoing pants and wearing a heavy sweater under his diving suit. When all was ready, lead shoes and weighted belt strapped on, the helmet was carefully lowered over his head and given the quarter turn to lock it in place. The heavy bolts were tightened, and he was helped to the boat's side. I expected him

Greek sponge boats from Tarpon Springs with sponger preparing to dive. Note the canvas-covered air hose held by the deck hand standing next to the foremast shrouds. Photo by H. Wright, 1946; State Archives of Florida.

to walk down the ladder, but instead he jumped overboard feet first, the helmet bobbed a minute or two, and then, leaving a stream of bubbles behind, he sank from sight. I later found that no self-respecting Greek diver ever descended the ladder.

As the diver hit bottom he started walking, the air hose, wrapped in white canvas, streaming out and upwards behind him. The engineer at the tiller followed the white hose and the stream of bubbles, adjusting the speed and direction to give the least pull on the diver and yet keep the air hose out from under the boat. The lifeline tender sat on the starboard bow holding the slender lifeline in his fingers, waiting for signals from below.

In a few minutes the diver signaled and the tender pulled on the line hand-over-hand until the sponge bag broke water.

Black, rubbery sponges were dumped on deck, and the bag was sent down again. An hour on the bottom and the diver bobbed to the surface and was pulled over to the ladder. He climbed heavily up to deck level, where the helmet was taken off before he climbed to the deck. I jumped aboard.

Niko pointed to the sponges, about the size of grapefruit.

"Sheepswool," he said. "Not very good and the bar is small. We're going to run up off Cedar Key to a reef I spotted last *gkasi*. You want to go down while we're getting ready?"

I was on the spot. They were friends, and they were both trying me out and offering me a chance not many but Greeks had ever had. I nodded. As he got out of his suit I was put in. It was cold and clammy, and I realized why the divers wore their sweaters. The lead shoes were strapped on, and I could hardly move my legs. The lead belt was fastened. Niko lifted the helmet.

"Wait a minute," I said. "I'm going to walk down that ladder."

"Okay, Voss," he nodded, "but take a hook with you. You know how to work the release valve?"

"Yes."

The helmet was put on, and the hiss of the air filled my ears. The suit started to inflate, and I pushed the valve on the side of the helmet with my head. Two divers helped me to the side of the boat, and I managed to get both feet over the side. I reached for the ladder, but Niko gave me a shove and I fell feet first into the Gulf.

As I shot underwater my chin hit the helmet plate and I thought for a minute I had broken both my jaw and my neck. The suit filled and the helmet bobbed above the surface. I looked up and there was Niko looking down with a grin on his face. He waved a hand and tilted his head.

Carefully I shoved against the air lever and sank into the dark green twilight gloom. My feet hit the bottom and I tried standing up. I blessed the lead shoes that now were not so heavy and kept me standing up. I walked forward slowly. The bottom was almost clear rock with big loggerhead sponges, low coral heads, and waving sea feathers reaching almost to my waist. The sponge hook reminded me, and I looked around.

It was hard for my inexperienced eye to tell a commercial sponge from a worthless one, but near my right foot was a sheepswool. I dug the hook into its base and gave a hard pull. It came off, but only with a good effort. With the sponge on the hook I looked up at the silvery surface above me, saw that I was well clear of the dark shape of the hull, and inflated my suit. Niko hauled me over to the ladder, and after several tries I got my feet on it and climbed to the level of the deck. He took the helmet off, handed it to a crew member, and helped me aboard. He looked at the sponge.

"You even got a sheepswool, but it's under size. See, it's slightly less than the width of the hook. You want us to clean it for you?"

I shook my head. I thanked them all, told them I would see them back in Tarpon Springs, and jumped aboard my own boat. Aboard the *mekanikos*, the propeller guard had been removed, the air hose coiled down, and the deck secured. All hands waved, and she turned northward, the inevitable sponge on the end of a long line dancing in her wake.

Every diving boat, by the time it cleared the harbor, had a sponge bouncing about in its wake. This puzzled me, and at last I asked what it was for, displaying my ignorance.

"Greek boats don't have a head," the diver told me. "We just sit on the taffrail and wash off with the sponge. It's much more sanitary, it's softer than the softest toilet paper, and it doesn't litter up the ocean."

The next morning, as we cleared the dock with the spongers watching, I sent one of the seamen aft and had him throw over a sponge on a line that I had gotten ready the night before. As it bobbed in the wake, the spongers laughed and waved. If sheep-swool sponges ever become popular, our new toilet paper television commercials will have to find something besides softness to talk about.

There are five or six different species of commercial sponges taken by the diving boats and a wider number of grades and varieties. An experienced diver or buyer can tell at a glance from the shape, texture, and color almost the exact reef where the sponge was taken.

Sponges are colonial animals, and the commercial sponges have a skeleton of protein—spongin—around and in which the fleshy tissue is found. The outer surface is tough and leathery, usually dark brown or black, and covered with fine pores through which the water is drawn and the microscopic food strained out. The water passes out of the sponge through large raised openings or oscula.

When the sponge is taken, it is first thrown into a pile with others in the sun and covered by wet sacking for the flesh to rot. When it reaches the right stage, it is taken out, squeezed, washed repeatedly in seawater, and then pounded and beaten with a wooden club until the animal matter is gone. The tough outer skin is hard to remove, and the remaining parts of this are scraped off with a short, wide-bladed knife. If the base has coral attached, it is pounded on a block with a wooden mallet until it is clean. Then the sponges are threaded with a giant needle in lines eight feet long and tied together in a "bunch." These are hung in the rigging and alternately dried out and wet and dried, again and again, to bleach out to a golden color. Only then are they ready to be stored in the Sponge Exchange waiting for the buyers from Pittsburgh or other sponge centers.

Sponge fishermen are not paid a salary but in shares, and

spongers are no exception to the rule that fishermen every-where are kept in debt one way or another. With the spongers, it is the financiers who own the boats or finance the building of one for a good captain. They own the ship chandlery also, and the captains and the crew have to buy from it.

Each crew member signs on for a certain number of shares, the largest going to the captain, the divers, and the engineer. There are usually two *taxidi* or cruises each year, of about five months each. At signing, each crew member gets an advance on his shares, an assignment of so much money a week to his family. Any money above this, if the cruise is successful, comes from the sale of the sponges and his share. Since the sponger has to buy from the financiers, who charge more than on the open market, there is seldom any money left in his pocket when the shares are paid out. Most likely the sponger is in debt, which ensures that he will sign on again.

Each *taxidi* is broken up into *gkasi*, intervals between refueling and reprovisioning stops, or because of bad weather. During short spells of bad weather the *kaikis* gather in the nearest shelter and wait for the wind to drop and the seas to run down. When working off Big Bank, the boats would congregate on the shallow bank and, using long anchor line scope, ride it out nested together for company.

When I was on Big Bank for shelter, I used my big bower anchor and 200 fathoms of line to keep the anchor from dragging in the mud and riding out onto the turtle grass. When the diving boats came running in and saw us securely anchored, several of them would ask permission to come alongside with fenders out. Snugged down, the crews would gather aboard one of the boats, a bottle of ouzo would appear, and the atmosphere in the cabin would get hazy with cigar smoke.

Then the tales would begin. One of the divers would translate, or perhaps all would speak in English. Many of them had escaped from Greece and would tell of narrow escapes from

Italian and German patrols. There were several Italians in the crews, and they were good-naturedly joshed about the inability of the Italian army to control the Greeks, but Germans were cordially hated. The Greeks suffered horribly in World War II, and even worse was awaiting some of those who eventually went home.

During one blow I was invited aboard one of the *kaikis*. In the cabin a silent group of men was gathered around one of the engineers. A small dark man, he had a ruler, a pad of paper, and a pencil. He was making a sketch, I thought, of the man in the bunk opposite. I was amazed to see that the man in the bunk had an erection, and that the little man was taking measurements of his penis with a piece of string and recording them on the pad. As I watched he took the length of the shaft and the glans, wrapped the string deftly around to get the circumference, plotted these out on the pad, and rapidly sketched in the outline and details with careful minuteness. When he was finished the man in the bunk pulled up his baggy sea trousers and grinned at me. He reached behind the bunk for a wad of bills and paid the artist.

"What in hell is going on?" I asked. There was a round of laughter. The friend who had invited me over said, "Aristides, show him one of your carvings."

The little man reached into a bag beside him and withdrew an object wrapped in cloth. He handed it to me. I unwrapped it, and there was a wooden phallus complete with scrotum, carved in dark wood and polished to a fine lustre. Every detail was carved with care, the work of a master. One of the divers sitting forward pointed at his chest with pride, "That's me."

"But what do you do with them?" I asked.

"Well," one explained, "we're gone to sea for five months. I give it to my wife who misses me, and she thinks only of me every time she looks at it. Good idea, *ne?*"

I wrapped it up and handed it back. The little man grinned and pulled out his string and a ruler. "How about it, you want one too?"

"I think I'll have a glass of ouzo instead, *evcharisto*." Everyone laughed again, and the inevitable stories started their rounds.

While the divers are always in some danger, sharks do not necessarily count large. They seem most interested in the diver's white hands. If a nosy shark approaches, the diver puts his hands under his armpits, inflates his suit, and blows bubbles at the creature if it comes too near. Sea turtles, on the other hand, particularly loggerheads, have been known to cut the white air hose in two. In eight to nine fathoms a diver can hardly be brought to the surface fast enough to save him as the pressure forces his body into the helmet. Divers seldom get the bends.

There was an old man who was watchman at one of the boat yards who spent much of his time sitting in the sun reading his Bible. When he got up to go down past the boats and curio stores on Dodecanesi Avenue, he walked nearly bent at right angles and was pointed out to the tourists as a former diver who had gotten the bends. I asked George, one of the divers, about him.

He laughed. "Diver nothing, he's never been in a suit. He was a coal miner in Pennsylvania and got the bends in a pit head. That's just a story everyone tells the tourists. They love it and they pay him to let them take his picture."

Even in those days the divers seldom worked below eight fathoms. But there were stories of the fabled early Tarpon Springs divers who worked to twelve to fifteen fathoms. That was dangerous work. Over and over again, however, divers told me that back on the Alexandria Banks, where many of them had learned their trade, skin divers wearing only goggles and nose clips had worked to forty-two fathoms. That is 252 feet, and I did not believe it. To my doubts they would say that the water was "different" in the Mediterranean, and that it was true. But pressure is pressure, and it increases by one atmosphere with each thirty feet in depth.

One evening I was sitting at a table with some of my friends at a reception for the archbishop of America, Athenagoras, later to become the *papas* or pope of the Greek Orthodox Church. He was sitting at the next table with some local dignitaries. One of the divers leaned over.

"Voss," he said, "the archbishop was once the 'sponge priest' of Alexandria. Would you believe him if he told you that the divers could go to forty-two fathoms on the Alexandria Banks?"

"It would be convincing," I replied.

After the dinner was over, the diver introduced me to Archbishop Athenagoras. "How deep could the naked divers dive off Alexandria, *kyrie*?" he asked.

"Forty-two fathoms," came back the answer immediately.

"But," he added as he saw my puzzlement, "those divers were life-term prisoners from jails on the Greek islands. They were offered their freedom if they made a certain number of dives. They went down holding onto a weight. They went down fast, hooked sponges off the bottom in beds so thick that all they had to do was reach out in any direction and pull them in, yanked on their lifeline, and were pulled to the surface by two men as fast as they could heave them in. Many of them died after a few dives, but others lived and were freed and became regular divers. But never again at that depth. Only prisoners dived for their lives."

Later I found a full account of this diving in one of the standard fisheries treatises.

Several curio stores faced the wheelhouse of my boat when it was at the base. My regular berth was just to the rear and to the side of the St. Nicholas Curio Store. The stores across the street were kept by young Greek girls who were mainly chosen for their good looks. They were beautiful, dark-haired and dark-eyed, and they sat in front of their stores chatting back and forth while waiting for customers.

My gunner's mate used to sit by the hour watching the girls through the binoculars.[4] One day Bill Moutsatsos, the baker, noticed this and turned to one of the girls.

"Have you heard about the new kind of binoculars that the Coast Guard has now?"

The girls shook their black tresses and looked toward the wheelhouse, where Simmons was watching them.

"Yes," Bill continued, "it has some kind of new type of glass and a built-in ray that passes right through brick or stucco or wood or even metal so that they can see what people are doing inside."

One of the girls looked at him, eyes widening. "Can it see through cloth?"

"Of course, it . . ."

With a volley of screams the girls fled into the dark interiors of their shops. Simmons put down the glasses.

"I wonder what the hell happened. All the girls screamed and ran inside and Bill is doubled up laughing on the sidewalk."

For two days not a girl appeared outside the shops. They looked wrathfully at Simmons and me when we tried to talk to them, and they edged away. Finally I asked Bill what had happened and he told me the story.

"Well, you're breaking the hearts of all of those girl watchers on the patrol boats. I think you should do something."

Bill did, and that afternoon the girls sheepishly returned to the sidewalk gatherings, but for weeks they blushed and looked uncomfortable every time they saw a pair of binoculars turned their way.

Besides the diving boats or *mekanikos*, Tarpon Springs also had a fleet of sponge hookers. Most of these were sloops, beautifully proportioned with graceful sheer, bowsprits, and big gaff-headed main sails. They were brightly painted, and as they sailed down the river they towed behind them a long line of dinghies. Long sponge poles lay in racks along the side, each pole fitted on the end with three-tined hooks.

Out on Big Bank in good weather we could see the sloops at anchor or lying with their dinghies out over the bank. There were two men in each dinghy. The oarsman sat or stood and rowed facing forward—brosing, as it was called—slowly moving the boat over the bottom. The hooker kneeled in the bow, his chest resting against the padded gunwale, peering over the side with a glass-bottomed bucket. The sponge hook rested by his hand, the long pole supported in a high crotch in the stern. Twenty or thirty feet down a sponge would come into view, and the hook would slide overboard. As the tines came down in front of the sponge, the hook was embedded in it and the pole was jerked back. The bucket, fastened to the gunwale by a short line, was dropped; the hook was raised; and the sponge was removed and thrown in the bottom of the boat. The water was dumped out of the bucket, and the search went on. It was backbreaking work. The shallow waters were restricted solely to hooking, and diving boats were arrested if caught with a diver over the side in those waters.

This was the type of sponging that I was familiar with and had done in the Keys. The Key Westers and the conchs swore that the lead shoes of the divers tramping on the bottom killed young sponges, and no diving was permitted south of the Ten Thousand Islands. Occasionally a Greek diving boat would get into Key West territory and then the sponge boats were burned, some Greeks were killed, and there were fights even in Key West itself.

Actually it is doubtful whether the divers' shoes did any harm, and because sponges can regenerate from bits and pieces, it is even possible that the shoes aided in forming new sponges.

A man from the State Board of Conservation cruised around the banks checking the sizes of the sponges taken by the hookers. He carried a brass ring four inches in diameter. If a sponge could drop through without touching both sides, it was undersize and illegal. On one cruise his boat broke down. I was then in charge of a fast cabin cruiser about 48 feet long, and I was ordered to take the inspector on his rounds. A few illegal sponges were found and confiscated. As the inspection went along I began to be surprised at the lack of any attempt to hide the small sponges and the willingness with which spongers gave them up.

The inspector told me that thousands of illegal sponges were taken out of Tarpon Springs each year, hidden away in various articles. He took a Prince Albert tobacco can and proceeded to shove silk sponge after silk sponge, each about four inches in diameter, into the can and finally closed the lid. He handed it to me.

"Now take them out."

I did, and I was surprised at the size of the pile of sponges pulled out of the can.

"Those crooked Greeks can take a fortune in sponges out of the state hidden away in a car going north. And they do it all the time. I know there are more illegal sponges hidden away on those boats, but I could spend months searching them and never find them all. No sir, that's a bunch of crooked Greeks."

His eyes glinted with satisfaction at the growing piles of sponges we had confiscated. I wondered just how many of those sponges ever saw the state conservation headquarters. He started stuffing the sponges back into the Prince Albert tobacco can, of which I noticed that he seemed to have a good many at hand. Yes, I thought, crooked Greeks indeed. If they were, they sure had a lot of company.

8

~~~~~~~~~~

The Viveros

*Preserving the catch in marketable condition has always
been a problem for commercial fishermen far from their
home port, a problem for which there were only three
traditional solutions: salt, live wells, and ice. Salt was used
as a preservative for thousands of years, but salt fish makes
grim eating (the centuries-old salt cod industry of the
North Atlantic was only sustained by religious observance),
and until the invention of cheap manufactured ice early
in the 1900s, the only inexpensive way to get fresh fish
to market from distant fishing grounds was in live wells.
Live-well fishing schooners were once common in the Gulf
of Mexico, but by the mid-1900s they were still used only
by Cuban fishermen.*

*Live wells were located amidships and were enclosed
by two thick watertight bulkheads extending from
keelson to deck and from the port to the starboard side
of the hull. A third bulkhead sometimes supported the
deck and divided the well into two compartments, each
with its own hatchway. Sea water circulated through the
live well through hundreds of auger holes, each an inch
or two in diameter, that were bored directly through the
hull.[1]*

R.S.V

The Gulf was oily calm, the surface like burnished steel. Overhead the sun was hot and angry in a blue sky that deepened to purple near the sea's edge, so that the sea and sky were one. A hundred yards away a long, blue-hulled schooner, her sails furled, rolled in the swell, her topmasts forming long parabolas against the sky. A line of men stood by the weather rail hauling fishing lines up from the deep. A big red and silver fish rose struggling from the sea and disappeared into the schooner's bowels.

Painted on the vessel's bow was her name, ALONZO PINZON, and as we rounded up under her lee counter I could see her hailing port, La Habana. A small, wiry, deeply tanned man wearing a tasseled watch cap stood at her taffrail watching us.

I waved. "Buenos días, capitán. Quiero su permisión venir a bordo."

He looked me over. I was barefoot, wearing faded dungarees, a white skivvy shirt, and a straw hat. I did not look like a boarding officer, but the heavy guard belt and holstered .45 was all the authority he needed.

He waved back. "A su gusto . . ." (he hesitated for the proper military title) ". . . señor," he finished lamely.

As the seaman brought the patrol boat up, I waited for the right roll of the schooner and jumped to the bulwark, catching the main backstay for support. I dropped to the silvery bleached deck as one of my men, in uniform, followed me, his leather-soled regulation shoes slipping on the cap rail.

In broken Spanish, assisted by the fragmentary English of the captain, or *patrón*, as fishing boat captains were called, I explained that I had to search his vessel for aliens and contraband. He waved his arm toward the waist of the schooner. "A su gusto, at your pleasure," he repeated and stepped aside.

I had never been aboard a Cuban *vivero* or live-well grouper and snapper smack before. She was a big schooner, about 120 feet long, and I knew beyond a doubt that she was not Cuban-built but a bluenose or Newfoundland Grand Banker. The after cabin was low and occupied much of the space from the main mast aft and gave some protection to the helmsman. Forward of the main mast the deck was flush except for a low coaming around the main hatch. Forward of the foremast was the hatch leading down into the crew's quarters in the fo'c'sle. There were dinghies sitting in their chocks on each side of the after cabin and one in the davits over the stern.

The fishermen eyed me curiously but never missed a haul as I walked forward and looked into the main hatch. The entire hold was one gigantic live well, with dozens of red snapper and grouper milling around. Refrigeration was virtually unknown in Cuba in those days, so cooks and housewives demanded their fish alive from the cages along the seawall at the old fish market in Havana. Hence the big *viveros*.

The cap rails on the bulwarks were deeply cut from the years of hauling bottom lines across them. As I watched, a fisherman was hauling his line across the cap rail hand-over-hand. There was a pause, then he swung a 20-pound grouper onto the deck. It lay flopping with belly distended, mouth open, and its swim bladder sticking out of its mouth. It would never live to swim in the live well, I thought.

But the fisherman reached for a sheath at his belt, pulled out a polished wooden object with a projecting tube, and jabbed it into the fish's side. There was a gush of air, the belly contracted, the swim bladder disappeared, and the mouth closed. The fisherman kicked the fish into the live well, where it floated for a moment, then gave a flip of its tail and joined its fellows in the milling crowd.

"Well, I'll be damned," I said in amazement. I tried to see the tube; the *patrón* handed it to me. It was a wooden handle of madeira, about an inch wide and six inches long, with a brass tube that ran through it and projected out one end about six inches. The projecting end was cut on a slant, like a lancet, and was

ıban live-well schooner (*vivero*) viewed from the stern of a Coast Guard patrol boat
f Anclote Key. Photo by G. L. Voss, 1943.

sharp as a needle. I returned it, and the fisherman stuck it back in the sheath.

"Doesn't that kill a lot of fish?" I asked.

The captain shook his head. "No, very few die, and if they do we split them and salt them. Nothing is lost."

Pulling a fish up rapidly from even 10 fathoms releases the pressure so fast that a fish has no time to reabsorb the gases in its swim bladder, which expands, actually causing the fish to come to the surface more rapidly as it becomes more buoyant. At the surface, if the bladder is too expanded, the fish will die; if it is only slightly expanded, the fish may resorb the gases and live. The puncture tube, or pricker, as it was called, was an ingenious gadget.

With a seaman to help, and accompanied by the *patrón*, we searched the vessel from the forepeak to the lazarette. The crew's quarters were crowded, the berths about six by four feet and built into the sides. Personal gear was stored in sea bags or small sea chests. Aft of the live well in the half deck were lockers and tubs full of fishing gear: new lines, leaders, sinkers and hooks. Barrels of salted fish were secured to the bulkheads. The after cabin had bunks for the captain, mate, and several of the senior fishermen.

If a vessel of this size were carrying contraband or drugs, only the most detailed search taking hours and involving opening the bilges and checking bulkheads would ever bring them to light. I knew it, and the *patrón* knew it, but the officers back in the district headquarters in Miami apparently did not. After all, they had never searched a schooner of this size. And what about the live well, and the fish, and the salt barrels?

When we had finished, I talked with the crew. The speech of Cuban fisherman is a far cry from classic Castilian or even formal South American Spanish. But of one thing I was certain: no German infiltrator could speak it well enough that the differences wouldn't be glaring.

When it was all over, I thanked the *patrón* for his time and cooperation.

"But now let's have a drink," he said.

"¡Bueno!," I replied.

The captain took a long pole with a hook on the end of it, reached under the fish hatch in the live well, felt around a moment, and with a smile pulled out a bottle of *añejo* rum. It had been hanging on a peg underwater, with no telling how many more, well hidden and cool. Wiping it off, he unscrewed the top, half-filled two coffee mugs, and handed one to me.

"¡Salud!" we said, almost together. *Añejo* is a great rum, and it slid down with ease. "¡Salud!" we said again on a more generous slug. I offered him a pack of American cigarettes, and he responded with a pack of strong Cuban ones, El Brazo Fuerte. After a third cup I thought I had better return while I could still make it from the heaving rail of the schooner to the bouncing deck of my patrol boat.

We departed with much waving of arms and *adioses* across the water. Ultimately the *patrón* of the ALONZO PINZON and I became quite well acquainted, as I had occasion to board her more than once, the exchange of civilities becoming more profuse on each trip.

For some reason known only to the powers that were at headquarters, the Coast Guard was convinced that aliens, and possibly German spies, were slipping in along the coast from the big Cuban *viveros*. The idea, apparently, was that the *viveros* turned them over to the Greeks, slipping in toward Big Bank at dark, and that the Greeks ran them in directly to Tarpon Springs or turned them over to smaller craft working out of the innumerable small creeks and rivers on the mangrove coast north of Tarpon Springs. This I do know, however: no Greek would have landed a German spy without first cutting his throat.

Perhaps this bureaucratic conviction was a holdover from Prohibition days, when the big schooners lay off the coast laden with rum or whisky and gave the Coast Guard fits. Drugs or other contraband were reportedly passed to small vessels and placed on the tops of the guano racks that lined the coast, to be picked up later by other boats that took it ashore. No one ever came near a guano rack except the collecting boat, so the platforms were probably safe places for such transfers.[2]

The Cuban *vivero* fishery had its beginnings around 1850 with live-well schooners fishing the banks off the west coast of Florida, the Middle Ground, and the Campeche Bank off Mexico. The original *viveros* were Cuban-built, but with the decline of the Grand Banks schooner fishery and the change to diesel-powered vessels, many Canadian schooners were sold to Cuban fishing companies for *viveros*. The ALONZO PINZON was one of these.

The *vivero* fishery was based mainly on two species, the red snapper or *pargo americano* (*Lutjanus campechanus*), and the red grouper or *cherna americana* (*Epinephelus morio*).[3] Havana *viveros* usually sailed first to the coast off Pinar del Río to catch sardines for bait with a pelagic trawl or *chinchorro*. On the snapper grounds the vessel was hove to (*a la capa*), and all hands fished. Occasionally, big jewfish upward of 500 pounds were caught. If these were thrown into the live well they would eat many of the smaller fish. To prevent this, the fishermen would wire the fish's jaws shut.

When fishing was good, a *vivero* might spend only two or three days on the fishing grounds and then set all sail for Havana for a quick run to market before the fish began to die. In Havana the catch was sold immediately. If there was a delay, the *vivero* would put back out to sea in clear, pure ocean water, because the harbor water was polluted and the fish would die if left in it for long.

The Cuban *viveros* at that time were spread out all over the Gulf of Mexico from the Florida coast to the Middle Ground and the Mexican banks. The *vivero* fishermen were a hardy lot, and they were great fishermen, but unfortunately they gave little heed to the careful upkeep of their standing rigging, as I found out to my near demise.

For some reason the commanding officer at the base at Tarpon Springs decided he wanted to make a boarding trip with us. He came aboard in starched and immaculately creased khakis, gold-striped shoulder boards, and a cap with shiny visor and gold braid.

We ran thirty miles offshore, and the first *vivero* came into view. I was barefoot and dressed in my usual seagoing dungarees, skivvy shirt, and straw hat. I reached into a drawer for my guard belt and started to buckle on the .45.

"Voss, you aren't going to board a foreign vessel dressed that way are you?"

"Sure, this way they aren't scared of me, and I can learn more from them," I replied.

"No man from my base will board a foreign vessel out of uniform," he declared. "You will dress properly."

There was no refusal. I quickly changed into dress whites, wrapped on leggings, buckled on the .45, and squared my hat. I looked at the old ALONZO PINZON and wondered what the *patrón* would think.

As we jumped aboard, the *patrón* raised an eyebrow but said nothing. Astern, my patrol boat lay off with a seaman at the forward machine gun covering us, all according to regulations.

I greeted the captain and introduced my commanding officer. "Es mi teniente," I explained. "El insista en las formalidades."

He nodded. "Sí, todos los oficiales son lo mismo."

When we had finished, and the lieutenant was watching the fishermen, the *patrón* motioned to me, and we went into his cabin, where he quietly poured me a cup of rum. "¡Salud!" he said and grimaced toward the officer. Cubans had no love for authority in uniform. "¡Salud!" I raised my cup and drained it; I didn't either.

Coastguardsmen at battle stations on the CG 42028, demonstrating the approve[d]
wartime procedure while approaching and boarding alien vessels. Photo by G. L. Vos[s],
1943.

We boarded four schooners that day. Standing on the deck of the last one, the lieutenant swept the horizon with his binoculars. Several more vessels were known to be in the vicinity, and the lieutenant suggested I send a man aloft to the masthead to look for the others. None of the men had ever been aloft, and they all demurred.

"How about you, Voss?" the lieutenant asked. "You're an old sailor, how about you going aloft?"

I was a big man and weighed about 195 pounds. I looked at the ratlines on the shrouds and wondered when they had last been checked. The Cubans were all small, wiry men, not much over 120 pounds. I wasn't going to be faced down by the brass, however, so I went over to the port shrouds and pulled on one of the ratlines.

"¿Están fuertes?" I asked the *patrón*. "Are they strong?"

"Sí, sí, muy fuertes," he replied.

I swung up onto the bulwark and tested the first ratline. It held. I looked up at the crosstrees 100 feet above me and started to climb. I didn't mind the height, but I still didn't trust the ratlines. With each step I took a firm grip on the shrouds. About 80 feet off the deck the ratline I was on suddenly parted. I hit two more, and they broke too, and I found myself hanging from the shrouds by my hands. The men far below were gaping with open mouths. I froze.

When my heart came back to normal and I could breathe again, I grabbed the backstay and climbed hand-over-hand to the crosstrees. From the masthead, the deck looked like a model, and the men were midgets. There was almost no swell, but even so the masthead swooped slowly from side to side as the boat rolled sluggishly.

I soon located another schooner through the binoculars and pointed her out to the deck, where a compass bearing was taken; then I slid to the deck by way of the backstay.

"No están fuertes," I told the *patrón*, pointing to the ratlines.

"Oh, no, señor, están muy fuertes, muy fuertes. ¿Verdad?" I wouldn't have trusted that fellow on a stack of Cuban Bibles.

When we reached the next schooner, the MANUELA out of Nuevitas, I couldn't see a sign of a fisherman. There was only one man on deck, presumably the captain. When we jumped aboard I asked him where the crew were. He pointed forward toward the main hatch. "Con los pescados, señor," he replied. "With the fish. The fish need more air or they will die."

I looked down into the live well, and there was the entire crew, swimming and thrashing about in the water, beating the surface to a froth. When there was no sea, the schooner did not roll, and there was no seawater exchange through the holes in the bottom of the hull. Without the exchange, the fish soon used up the available oxygen and suffocated. The *viveros* had no air or water pumps, so in calm weather the crew's thrashing oxygenated the water.

Cuban *viveros* were not the only vessels fishing for grouper and snapper on the Middle Ground. A number of Florida ports such as Pensacola, Port St. Joe, and Carrabelle had Middle Ground fishing fleets. Their schooners were much smaller than the Cuban boats, but none were so graceful, and the fish on them were gutted and iced.

On the following Sunday we had a call from one of the offshore cutters requesting a fast patrol boat to be sent out to a *vivero* off Anclote Key. A seaman had gone aloft to hand over a topsail sheet when the ratlines parted and he fell. He hit the bunt of the sail and fell into one of the dinghies. His weight and momentum carried him through a thwart and part way out of the bottom. He was wedged so tightly that they couldn't get him out, so he was transferred, dinghy and all, into the Coast Guard boat. He was finally cut loose in the hospital at Tarpon Springs.

9

Crystal River Oystermen

Florida has abounded in oysters since prehistoric times. Mute evidence of the productivity of the state's oyster beds are the vast shell mounds created by centuries of pre-Columbian seafood consumption on both coasts. South of Lake Okeechobee prehistoric shell mounds were the highest landscape features encountered by the early settlers, and they remained prominent local landmarks until bulldozed or excavated for fill. Statistics from the nineteenth-century oyster industry are almost equally impressive, and even as late as 1944 the Gulf Coast Florida fishery alone produced over 1.5 million pounds of oysters.

Commercially valuable oysters are found in shallow coastal waters near river mouths or in other inshore situations where the natural salinity of seawater is diluted by fresh water. On the Gulf Coast of Florida most oysters were harvested by "tonging" from small craft in water less than 10 feet deep. Oyster tongs resembled a pair of long garden rakes joined by a pivot about one-third of the way from the tines to the end of the shafts. The tongs used in Florida ranged from 10 to 16 feet long. Standing on the deck of his boat, the oysterman lowered the tongs in the open position onto the oyster bar and then worked the shafts back and forth until the rakes could be closed on one another by bringing the shafts together.

The tongs were then hauled hand-over-hand up onto the boat and the oysters released onto the deck for culling and sorting.[1]

R.S.V.

The fish house sat in the sedge with a narrow passage leading up to it. About a dozen open launches were moored to the dock, completely blocking it. I looked the place over from the after cockpit of the CG 42028. I had been sent to Crystal River to try to bring peace to an explosive situation between my Coast Guard predecessors and the local fishermen. The latter had threatened to kill any coastguardsman who interfered with them.

The harbor entrance boat I had relieved had gone by the book—dress whites, leggings, guard belt, and .45. The seamen were mostly from Brooklyn and looked down their noses at the "poor white trash" living in a Tobacco Road setting, and told them so.

"Poor white trash" has an opprobrious meaning in the South; they are fighting words. I had to impress the fishermen that I and my crew were different. My motor mac, Clyde Everett, was a big Texas cowboy with a slow, soft drawl, but the seamen were only six months out of the Bronx and boot camp.[2] By now Clyde and I had trained them well, and they were even eating grits. But what to do to break the hatred?

From the fish house half a dozen fishermen were eyeing us with disdain, but puzzled. We were in dungarees, and I was barefoot and wore a straw hat, my usual seagoing garb.

I put the wheel amidships with one engine ahead and the other astern. The long, gray-hulled cruiser slowly turned around as if on a pivot. As her stern swung across the opening in the sedge I put the other engine in reverse, and the boat slid into the channel with the sedge brushing both sides of the hull. The fishermen watched deadpan as the largest boat that had ever been to their dock backed slowly toward them, negotiated the dogleg, and stopped inches from the bows of their launches. The seamen swung the boats aside and held them clear. Again I backed down and cut the engines six inches from the wharf. I dropped a line on a piling, made it fast, and stepped onto the wharf.

"Morning," I took them all in. "Okay to lay here for a couple of hours while we get some groceries?"

No one said a word. One nodded toward a room in front with the word "Office" painted over the door. Sitting at a desk was a heavy-set man wearing suspenders and smoking a pipe. He looked up as I knocked. "Come in and have a seat."

"I'm in charge of the harbor entrance boat that has just taken over the duty. I'd like permission to lay here for an hour or two while a couple of my men go up town to get some groceries."

"I noticed you bring that boat in. Not much like the way that other fellow barged in. Where did you learn to handle a boat like that? Not in the Coast Guard."

"No," I replied. "I'm an ex-commercial fisherman and charter-boatman."

"Thought so. Sure, you can lay here, but unless there's another boat in, the dock over at the spring is clear and you'll be less bothered by my boats going in and out. Here, I can't control those fishermen if they get mad at you or your crew. They got pretty sore lately."

"I heard about that and can't say that I blame them. That's what I'm here for and there'll be no trouble from my men."

I shook hands, walked back past the hostile fishermen, and sent the two seamen up town with the grocery list. I sat down in the cockpit with Clyde to watch the fishermen.

When we arrived they had been looking at several mounds of new webbing piled near the door. Now one of them ran a long length of cork line and lead line from wall to wall, fastened to hooks on the timbers. To these lines they then loosely attached a mullet-net webbing and started to hang it in with net needles. There was an argument as to whether it should be hung stretched or full. In a few minutes I saw why, as they then strung two other lengths of webbing with large meshes about a foot square on each side of the mullet webbing. They were hanging in a trammel net. More argument. Did the trammel hang full or stretched? Do you hang first one and then the other?

A section was hung in, examined, cut back out, hung again, and more argument. Then the whole net was cut loose and they stood perplexed.

I stepped out onto the dock. "Hanging in a trammel net?" I asked. "Seem to be having a problem. Maybe I can help."

They stared at me and I could see the owner of the fish house get up and come to the door.

I picked up the mullet webbing. Without waiting for permission I took some short lengths of twine and attached the webbing at intervals to both lines. Then I did the same with both of the trammels. I held out my hand for the net needle. After a slight hesitation someone handed it to me.

I tied in, and as fast as I could I hung all three nets at the same time. I was halfway across the room on the cork line when the first fisherman came over to see how I was doing it. By the time I finished the cork line two others had joined me. I cut off and tied into the lead line. I tried to hand the needle to the net owner. He shook his head.

"You do a little more. I haven't quite got the hang of it."

They now all crowded around, and I explained the way to work. The mullet webbing must be hung full and loose, the trammels flat and stretched, so that the mullet webbing could go through with a fish and form a pocket to hold it. Questions started to flow. I unfastened the finished section and everyone started to help set up the new lines and string the leads and corks. I fastened the webbing on the cork line while one of the others fastened the lead line. I gave him the needle. As he started to hang in I advised and demonstrated a couple of times, and he got the knack. I walked back to the wharf edge and sat down on a piling alongside Clyde. One of the fishermen reached into the icebox and got a couple of beers. "You and your buddy like one?"

In another half hour Clyde was regaling them with tall Texan tales, we had been invited to the dance that weekend at the schoolhouse, and we'd made at least six friends. As we pulled out of the tangle of boats in the early afternoon, beer bottles were waved in goodbye.

The next morning, just after dawn, the first oystermen came by. The twenty-foot launch, unpainted, and built of great wide cypress planks, heaved and panted with each revolution of the ancient two-cylinder engine. Strung out astern were six big flatties that immediately wrapped themselves around us when the motorboat stopped alongside our stern. There were two men in each flattie, and oyster tongs were hanging over the bow.

I looked into the launch and saw what had been causing all the trouble. We were supposed to check not only the fuel and number of men in each crew, but also the proper boat equipment. But there was no fire extinguisher—only a bucket of sand. And for life preservers there was a stack of three-inch-thick two-by-four-foot-long cypress planks with a hand-hold in each end. I didn't even try to look for a horn.

"You've got to have an approved fire extinguisher and regulation life jackets. There's no way I can pass this equipment."

"I don't see why for we need new ones. These are the same kind my pappy and my grandpappy used," the oysterman told me. "I ain't got no money for them things."

"Well, you've got to have them."

"That's what them other fellows said that were here. Maybe the oyster house will buy them. If'n I have to get them I'll have to quit oystering."

I let them go, and they chugged on out the river toward the

Florida Gulf Coast oystermen using tongs. Photographer unknown, 1946; State Archives of Florida.

maze of oyster bars that nearly blocked the channel and spread for miles on either side. All the other boats that came by had the same equipment, and I repeated my instructions. I had real sympathy for them. They were hardworking, underpaid people, living on the thin edge of subsistence. Until the war came along and the Coast Guard was stationed at the river, no one had ever boarded them or inspected one of their boats. They never went offshore, but worked around the oyster bars in protected water. What need was there for these expensive pieces of gear?

The fire extinguisher would never be rechecked or refilled, and the life jackets would get torn and ruined before a year was out, while the cypress planks were practically indestructible, although as weathered and soaked as they were, they might not even float in the unlikely event that one was ever needed. I could understand the men's sullen looks as they checked back in that evening. I never made another equipment check while I was at Crystal River, and I doubt if a single fire extinguisher or life jacket was ever bought. When the boatmen found that we were not going to bother them, they began to wave as they went by. After all, there were no German spies hanging around the oyster bars waiting to be smuggled ashore by the oystermen.

The weekend dance was a great success. We got invitations to other affairs and even to go hunting with one of the local ranchers, King Smith. The Big Gulf Hammock was a wilderness then, filled with deer, bears, panthers, and wild turkeys. The hunting was excellent, but the results were poor.

Our station at the river mouth was at a pair of dolphins or cluster pilings, lying about midway between Shell Island and the mainland. Shell Island was a low island covered with cabbage palms and tangled shrubbery. Like most such islands, it was a haven for rattlesnakes.

One morning, after the oystermen had cleared the river mouth, Clyde and I were sitting on the starboard gunwale of the cockpit and Clyde was stringing the two seamen a wild tale of his period of duty in the Ten Thousand Islands and up the Shark River at Cape Sable. Groceries had run low or run out, and they were reduced to eating various birds, fish, and 'possum. The tale got wilder, and he launched into how they were bothered with snakes dropping off overhanging limbs onto the deck. At night they had to set a watch to kill the snakes and prevent them from crawling into the scuppers.

"Oh, come off it, Clyde," I had just started to remonstrate, when he dug me in the ribs with his elbow and nodded his head back toward Shell Island. I glanced around and there was a big rattlesnake swimming toward us, its head held a few inches above the surface of the water. Its route would take it right along the side of the boat, and beside Clyde's foot was the cockpit scupper.

Clyde continued his story: "Yessir, those suckers would swim right along the side of the boat . . ." (I saw the snake pass by where we were sitting, its head gliding along the side of the boat) " . . . and they'd crawl right into those scuppers." The rattler thrust its head into the dark hole of the scupper. "And they'd crawl right into the cockpit." The snake's head stuck through about four inches. "By God, there's one right now!" Clyde raised his foot, clad in a high-heeled cowboy boot, and smashed the rattlesnake's head.

The two seamen nearly fell overboard, their faces white, and for once two Brooklyn boys were speechless. Clyde calmly reached down and pulled the rest of the snake through the scupper. It was a big fellow, nearly six feet long. Clyde put a line around its neck, hung it from the after end of the cabin, and began to skin it.

Clyde could have told the two seamen that the moon was made of green cheese after that, and they would have believed him. Afterward, every evening, the two would drive plugs into the scuppers to keep the snakes out. We never saw another the whole time we were at Crystal River.

The waterfowl on Crystal River were unbelievable. Besides the usual wading birds, the surface of the river was literally covered from shore to shore with Florida mallards and coots. The coots I was familiar with on the east coast were usually fishy-flavored and rather poor eating. But these on the river were so fat they could hardly get off the water, regular butterballs, and better eating by far than the ducks.

Coots were seldom shot, I was told. "We fram them."

"You what?"

"We fram them. One man sits in the bow of an outboard boat, and as the other runs through the coots, the man in the bow frams the water ahead with the pole. Then they turn around and pick them up."

I didn't believe it, but later I saw framming done and even did some myself. We always kept the icebox filled with coots and gave the ducks away on our infrequent relief trips back to Tarpon Springs.

One morning just after daybreak I walked up town from our berth at the city dock to mail some letters. Something big and black was hanging from the front of one of the stores. It was a bear.

"Found him eating a hog he'd killed, right in the middle of the street," the chief of police told me. "I don't want no hog-killing bear around here. No telling what he'd kill next."

When I next visited Crystal River long after the war, coots, ducks, and black bears were gone, never to return, their places taken by a Holiday Inn, motels, and marinas. Trammel nets and coot framming were things of the past.

10

~~~~~~

Cedar Key

*Green turtles are great eating, and there were once enough
of them to support a thriving fishery. So-called because
of the green fat (or calipee) found under the upper shell,
greens are one of five species of sea turtle found in Florida
waters, along with the loggerhead, hawksbill, ridley, and
leatherback. Uniquely, green turtles are herbivorous as
adults, grazing on marine plants (especially the aptly
named turtle grass) in shallow bays and river mouths,
where they were formerly taken in tangle nets. These nets
averaged about 100 yards long with huge mesh—18 to 24
inches, stretched—and they were anchored in likely places
overnight. The lead line was only lightly weighted to allow
entangled turtles to come up to the surface to breathe. In
the West Indies, and perhaps also in Florida, turtle nets
were sometimes provided with floating decoys carved
and painted like turtles to attract amorous males in the
breeding season.*

*Turtles were formerly abundant in the state. At Indian
River one fisherman reported catching 2,500 turtles with
eight nets in 1886. By the 1940s, however, the Florida
turtle fishery was not very productive. The huge pens (or
"crawls") next to the turtle canneries in Key West were
mostly stocked with turtles captured elsewhere, in the
West Indies or along the coast of Central America. One*

*of the last viable Florida fisheries for green turtles was
at Cedar Key.*[1]

R.S.V.

"I want that there feller for foolin' round with my girl. If'n you all don' hand him over, me and my boys goin' to come aboard and get him."

The tall, gaunt, grizzle-faced cracker mullet fisherman and his two lanky sons shifted their shotguns nervously. My four crewmen were standing together forward of the wheelhouse eyeing the guns apprehensively. They heaved a collective sigh of relief when they saw me come down the pier.

"What's the matter?" I asked the fisherman.

"That there feller," he said, pointing to one of the seamen, "been foolin' around my girl. She's a good girl and I don' want no strangers foolin' with her. He's goin' to come out on the dock here where my sons goin' to give him a thrashin' for foolin' round with their sister." He spat a load of tobacco juice onto the city wharf. "If'n he don' come out I'm goin' to shoot him right there."

"What happened, Bill?" I asked the supposed culprit.

"I just met the girl at the drugstore when the ice cream truck came in, and we had a dish of ice cream together. Then this fellow came along, grabbed her out of her chair, and threatened to beat me up. I came back to the ship and these three fellows came down."

The father raised his shotgun and pulled one of the hammers back. "Ain't nobody goin' to fool around with my girl," he repeated.

"Simmons, take the cover off that machine gun," I ordered my gunner's mate. The big water-cooled .50-caliber looked enormous. "Now cock it."

The three pulls on the cocking bar sounded like thunder in the sudden quiet on the pier. The three crackers looked bug-eyed at the big shells going into the block.

"Now, if either one of these three men makes a move with his shotgun or attempts to board the boat, fire. That's an order."

I turned to the fishermen. "You heard my order. If that girl of yours is as good as you say, you don't need to worry about her. If she isn't, my seaman still hasn't done anything, and it sure isn't wrong to buy a girl a dish of ice cream. Now you get the hell off this dock, clear out, and if I ever see any of you threaten a coastguardsman again I'll have you arrested and in jail before you know what's happened."

Simmons swung the muzzle back and forth across the three. Without a word they lowered their shotguns and walked away. I jumped aboard. Simmons unloaded the machine gun and put the cover back on. A diving boat was moored alongside, and the Greeks had been watching apprehensively. I didn't blame them; Greeks and Cedar Key crackers did not mix well. The spongers were getting ready to put to sea, and when they left I followed them down the channel past Seahorse Key.

In the late 1930s my oldest brother was the Methodist minister at Cedar Key. This was shortly after the crew of a Greek sponge boat had been arrested for supposedly molesting a Cedar Key woman; they were locked in the town jail and then lynched. Several of my brother's congregation had taken part in the lynching, and in one of his sermons he had preached against lawlessness. A delegation had quietly warned him that the subject was not one for discussion. While I was in Tarpon Springs the courts finally awarded each of the widows $35,000 compensation for their husbands' deaths. Cedar Key was not a good place to philander in, at least for outsiders.[2]

The town had once been a thriving port, one of the largest

Street scene in Cedar Key. Photographer unknown, 1949; State Archives of
Florida.

in Florida, the terminus of the Florida Railroad, the site of the
largest red cedar mill in the country (supplying the Faber Pencil Company), and the main center of the green turtle trade. All
that was left by the 1930s were the straggling remnants of the
cedar mill, oyster and mullet fishing, a little offshore grouper
fishing, and a local turtle fishery.

Turtles were caught in turtle nets, giant nets that were set
from point to point across the major bights. Green turtles were
regularly shipped from the town, and delicious turtle steaks were
served at the hotel near the wharf. With the complete protection
of the green turtle in later years, this industry also failed.

One noon I walked up to the pool hall and saloon. The bartender was about to close up as I walked in.

"Closing up?" I asked.

"Not just yet. What can I serve you?"

I just wanted to have a beer and knock the balls around for an hour or so. It was an old-fashioned pool table with green drapes to the floor. I finally racked the balls and leaned the cue stick against the wall.

"See you later," I said. As I walked out, he closed up.

It was about an hour before I got back to the boat. Everyone was excited.

"Have you heard about the bartender at the pool hall?" they asked.

"No, what about him?"

"He shot a man in an argument at the bar. He was just closing down to turn himself in when he saw a coastguardsman coming and put the dead man under the pool table. He's in the jail now."

They looked at me. "What's the matter?"

"Good Lord, I just came from there. I was shooting pool at the table with the dead man underneath. The bartender was locking up when I left."

We put right out to sea, and I was never called as a witness. Because the man who was shot was a drifter from Georgia, the bartender was released.

My wife and daughter and I recently drove over to Cedar Key for the afternoon. The town didn't look much different than it did during the war. I could not find the pool hall, and there were no diving boats in port. It was low tide, and a mullet fisherman was hauling his net but didn't have much. The oyster bars were bared, and launches were lying about on the mud flats. There was a shrimper moored to the city pier. A small artists' colony had invaded the island, but the paintings displayed for sale were not much to look at.

There is a historical museum near the dock. I pored through the news section looking for the Greek affair and the bar-room shooting. There was no mention of either. Cedar Key has become respectable, or at least it's trying. But I'd still make sure that girl you talked to was from out of town.

11

Filimingo, by God

In late 1944 Gil was transferred from coastal patrol duty to serve on the USS LCI(L)-90, a Coast Guard–crewed landing craft that had previously seen action during the invasions of Sicily and Normandy. One hundred and fifty-eight feet long, she was armed with four single-mount 20 mm anti-aircraft cannon and two .50-caliber machine guns. Gil reported aboard on November 17, 1944, at Charleston, South Carolina, where the ship was being refitted in the Navy Yard for service in the Pacific theatre. From Charleston the LCI(L)-90 proceeded via Key West and the Panama Canal to San Diego for training exercises. On April 20, 1945, she departed San Diego for Pearl Harbor, and from Pearl Harbor she stopped at Eniwetok, Guam, Ulithi, and Leyte on her way to Okinawa, where she arrived on May 29. On June 3, while participating in the invasion of Okinawa at Chimu Wan, the ship was hit by a Japanese suicide plane, which caused several casualties and considerable damage. The LCI(L)-90 immediately departed Okinawa for repairs at Leyte, where she and her crew remained, preparing to take part in the invasion of Japan, until the war ended only two months later.

Gil was honorably discharged from the Coast Guard in December 1945 and worked at a number of odd jobs in and around Hypoluxo in the first few months of 1946.

Gil at his battle station behind one of the 20 mm anti-aircraft guns on LCI(L)-90, somewhere in the Pacific. Photographer unknown, 1945.

One gets the sense that the ex-coastguardsman was somewhat at loose ends, with no clear idea about what to do next. Then brother Frederick turned up with a scheme that, in the event, would be Gil's last attempt to earn a living at fishing.

It is perhaps unsurprising that it took a genius like Alexander Graham Bell to conceive the idea of attaching an airplane propeller to a jon boat, but it is not recorded whether Dr. Bell was reckless enough to make the first experiment himself. Originally developed in Canada around 1905, airboats were introduced to Florida in the 1920s, where they soon became popular among mullet fishermen working the shallow bays of the southwest coast. Most of the early airboats were homemade affairs that entirely lacked any of the basic safety features—such as propeller cages—that are now standard equipment. There must have been numerous accidents, but those were less fretful times, and the survivors simply carried on.

R.S.V.

The other day my wife and I drove down to Flamingo. If you don't know where that is, look at a map and find the southernmost tip of Florida, Cape Sable. Just northeast of the cape, sitting on a marl mud flat, is what was once the wildest frontier town in the country. Today it is the end of the road in the Everglades National Park.

As the road cuts across the Flamingo Canal it turns left to a modern small-boat marina, a two-story building on stilts housing the Visitor's Center, and a motel. There are a few campsites in the open, surrounded by some starved coconut trees and stunted shrubs. A seawall runs in front of the buildings. The water is turbid. Across the waters of the bay are a few mangrove islands. That is Flamingo today.

In the Visitor's Center you can view exhibits on the local wildlife, the food chain of the birds and the mangroves, what hurricanes did to the cape, and a picture or two of the former village of Flamingo before it became a part of the park. On the second floor you can also see the high-water mark left by Hurricane Donna.

But you will see no trace of the old buildings or the colorful characters who lived, fished, fought, and moonshined in the little village of Flamingo, called Filimingo by its occupants before the government took it over. In fairness, though, if the park service had not destroyed the village, Hurricane Donna probably would have.

Flamingo and Cape Sable were names familiar to me long before I set foot there. In those shallow inshore waters Guy Bradley, the first Audubon warden, had been shot to death by his next-door neighbor, a plume hunter, as he tried to protect the bird rookeries. Guy had grown up on Lake Worth and had been one of my mother's childhood playmates. On a shelling trip when I was sixteen I saw his grave marker standing desolate in the wire grass on East Cape, seen by none but wandering fishermen and raccoons hunting for turtle eggs on the sandy beach.[1]

I first visited Flamingo in 1946, when I was just back from the Philippines and Okinawa with my discharge money. My brother Frederick persuaded me to chip in as a partner in a rig for mullet fishing at Cape Sable. According to him there were mullet there by the millions. Some Filimingos declared that if a mullet rallied, or showered out of the water in Flamingo, they would rally all the way to the Keys.

We bought a government surplus airboat and mounted a six-cylinder Chevrolet car engine on an iron frame in the stern. A stub shaft made in a local machine shop enabled us to attach a square-bladed airplane propeller to the crankshaft. A big plywood rudder was mounted behind the propeller, and we were in business. We tried the boat out in Lake Worth, and even in deep water she skimmed the surface like a seaplane about to take off.

"You take her out so I can get a picture of her," Fred told me.

I had never run an airboat before. I took off from the dock and ran downwind. The boat almost flew. When the time came to turn around, the wind had me, and all we did was go broadside across the lake at the same speed. I cut the motor, the boat settled into the water still going broadside at 20 miles an hour, and over we went. With that propeller still turning only a few feet away, I wrapped my arms around the engine frame and did not let go until I saw daylight overhead. I swam up and sat on the overturned hull. I had the dubious distinction of being perhaps the only person to turn an airboat over in deep water.

With the engine dried out and running again, all was in order. A few days later we headed for Cape Sable in our sea skiff, towing the airboat and net flattie behind us. Below Blackwater Sound we

turned westward and threaded the maze of channels, bars, and islets known only to Travis McGee and the BUSTED FLUSH.[2] We passed Madeira Bay and Snake Bight and finally reached our future home at Andrews' fish camp on the south bank of the Flamingo Canal, about where the bridge crosses the canal today.[3]

Flamingo was not much to look at. The "town" consisted of about a dozen weathered houses sitting on stilts eight to ten feet high on the eastern edge of a wet marl prairie with a few scrubby bushes. Along the waterfront were several larger buildings, the fish houses owned by Barrelhead and Mr. Roberts, and a number of long one- or two-plank docks on mangrove pilings running out into the shallow waters of the bay. Several of the houses were larger than the others, and near the south end was the old Bradley house. Guy's father had been the agent for the Model Land Company that owned the cape and had dug the drainage canals.

The waterfront at old Flamingo, with mullet gill nets drying on racks in the foreground. Photographer unknown, after 1947; courtesy of the National Park Service, Everglades National Park (EVER 307218).

A number of white-hulled launches were moored to the finger piers or anchored in water deep enough to float them at low tide. A single marl road ran from the wooden bridge across the canal down along the water past the fish houses to disappear in the scrub to the southward.

The launches used by the Flamingo fishermen were called "wheel boats"; that is, they were conventional boats with inboard engines and underwater propellers or "wheels." Going across the flats, these propellers dug out the turtle grass clear down to the bare marl, and the spidery wheel-boat trails crisscrossed Dildo Bank to the eastward.

Andrews' camp consisted of the fish house, built out over the canal edge, Andrews' home, and three or four new one-room cabins for the fishermen. On the opposite canal bank were the net racks for drying and mending the nets. Three other airboats were tied up in front of the cabins.

The road to Flamingo was a driver's nightmare. For most of the way from Florida City it was an unpaved rock road filled with deep holes and pits. It stretched on with hardly a turn for 30 miles, white and dazzling in the summer sun, bordered by elderberry bushes, scrub, and dwarfed mangroves. The road was so bad that it could wreck a car. Filimingos always drove the road on the left-hand side, putting the left wheels on the smooth bank and the right wheels on the unpitted crown. Driving on the left gave the driver a better measure of where his wheels were and how close he could get to the edge.

A Flamingo car could be recognized in Homestead or Florida City by the scratches on the left side and the comparatively untouched right side. Oddly enough, Filimingos did not pass each other on the left. As the cars neared, the drivers switched sides, then crossed again. This must have been very confusing to the few outsiders who ever ventured to Flamingo in those days.

We soon found that Flamingo wheelboatmen and airboatmen looked askance upon one another. The wheel boats fished the tides, locating mullet on the banks or in the channels at high tide and setting their nets downstream. When the tide ebbed, the mullet would gill in the nets as they sought deeper water. It meant fishing by the tide.

The airboats hunted for the mullet on the banks, ran the net around them, and pursed down until the fish hit the net. The airboatmen fished on any run of the tide. Naturally the wheel-boatmen said the airboats scared all the fish away, while the airboatmen complained that the wheel boat tracks in the turtle grass let all the mullet run out from beneath the lead line, swimming the trenches like traffic down the Dixie Highway. The wheel boats also tore so much turtle grass loose from the bottom that it often clogged the airboat nets and floated the lead line. Both parties were right to some extent.

My brother had fished before at the camp at Boggy Bight, just north of Flamingo, but for me our first day at work was an entirely new experience.[4]

We set out early in the morning with the net stacked in the stern of the flattie. There was a pole fastened to the end of the net, and it projected out over the side of the boat. Frederick would run the airboat and make the set. I was to jump overboard when he gave the signal, grab the pole out of the flattie as it went by, and ram it down in the mud. Frederick would then open the throttle and run the net around the school.

The water was like glass. We ran along at cruising speed, and occasionally there were swirls ahead as fish flipped downwards to escape the boat. Frederick kept telling me that the water was shallow and just to jump when he gave the word. Suddenly, ahead and to one side, the whole surface boiled.

"Jump!" he yelled.

I did. The water was not more than three feet deep, if that. I was anxious to keep clear of the propeller and tried to move sideways, but I couldn't. My legs were caught in two feet of soft, sticky marl. By now Frederick was speeding up, and I looked around just in time to see the flattie bearing down on me at 20 knots and about to run me down. I grabbed at the pole as it went by and managed to pull it out of the boat but could not hang onto it. Off went the flattie, skimming astern with the pole bobbing and thrashing around in the wake. Frederick circled the school, and it was only when he looked around to see how much of the net was left in the flattie that he saw me standing in the water waving my arms, with no sign of net floats bobbing in the water.

"What the hell happened?" he asked as he came by to pick me up.

"You were going so damned fast that I couldn't hold onto the pole, and besides, I'm stuck in the marl."

Back aboard and with the pole in the flattie, we started out again. A little later we saw another school, not as large as the first but worth setting. Again Frederick yelled, "Jump," and I went over the side. This time things went better; he kept the boat slowed down until I had the pole out and rammed into the bottom before he opened the throttle. The net ran out with a machine-gun rattle as the leads hit the stern of the flattie. The corks bobbed in the water in a nice circle as Frederick brought the airboat back and closed the net. Already we could see the cork line bobbing in places as mullet hit the webbing and gilled. A few jumped the cork line.

The airboat was now run in over the net, and the pole was lashed to it, the lower end tilted forward so that the lead line swept the bottom. With the engine idling we had just enough power to pull the net down slowly while we picked up into the flattie as we drew down onto the other end. As the circle became smaller, more and more of the fish jumped the cork line, and Frederick said we had better stop and corkscrew the net.

Now the net was full of two-foot-wide stingrays. To corkscrew the net we had to anchor the airboat, take the flattie with the net, and wade it around inside the circle in ever-smaller rings. I was not about to get into the water with all those sting-rays, but Frederick assured me that if I slid my feet along the bottom instead of lifting them, I would not get jabbed.

Very dubiously, I waded the flattie around until the circle was nearly filled with webbing. Both of us climbed into the flattie and began slamming the pole and an oar on the gunwales. This drove the mullet wild. They rallied, dived into the net, and we had the school. Mullet were bringing six cents a pound, and we finished with over 1,600 pounds in the boat: a successful first day of fishing. It was a performance that we were to repeat many times over the next months.

While we were clearing the net, a wheel boat came by and the fisherman asked how we had done. He was from Roberts' fish company, the main one in Flamingo.

There were three generations of Robertses. Back in the 1920s my father and his partner, my cousin Captain Walter Moore, had a charter for their 78-foot yacht, of which my father was engineer.[5] The cruise included a stop at Flamingo. Unfortunately, they had an engine breakdown and decided to leave the yacht for the day and go to Miami for the necessary parts. The only way to get there was by the big old touring car owned by the senior Roberts. He told them he was leaving bright and early in the morning, so they had best stay ashore that night and be put up in the spare room.

Cousin Walter remarked during the evening that there was nothing he would like better than a good drink of 'shine, but Roberts ventured nothing, and he went to bed thirsty. The next morning several dozen gallon jugs of white lightning were pulled from under the bed they had been sleeping in and were loaded into the old touring car for the trip to Miami. I don't think Cousin Walter ever forgave Mr. Roberts. Mr. Roberts, however, thought it was a great joke and laughed at Cousin Walter's "dry night."[6]

Saturdays were working days at Flamingo, but Saturday evening was the time to go to town in Homestead and drink the place dry. Late on Saturday afternoon several cars packed with passengers would head out up the dusty road.

The favorite saloon, at the south end of Homestead just across the railroad tracks, boasted the longest bar in Florida. Drinking began in earnest there, and when a few bottles had been downed, fights often broke out between the farmers and field hands from Homestead and the Filimingo fishermen. The fishermen were widely known for their bar-room techniques. Often, as a fight was about to start, it ended without a blow when the farmer asked where the other was from. The reply, "I'm from Filimingo, by God," was usually enough to end things before they started.

As the saloons closed, the Filimingos bought their bottles of booze and headed south for home. By the time the cars careened into Flamingo everyone was riding high, and yells and pistol, rifle, or shotgun blasts filled the night air, to the disadvantage of the corrugated tin roofs. With the liquor gone, there was nothing for it but to head north again for the Last Chance Liquor Store in Florida City. The cars ran back and forth all night, though less and less frequently into the early morning. By sunup the shouting and shooting died down until finally the whole town was asleep and tranquility reigned again.

All provisions were brought in from Homestead or Miami by the fishermen returning from days off or were ordered from the fish-truck drivers who shopped for the fish house before returning. Ice was to be had from the fish houses, but the local bill of fare was pretty dull, and it was enlivened only by fresh fish, mostly mullet, an occasional turtle, and once a week or so by a "purlo" of scrawk.

Scrawks came from Murray Key or Frank Key, just offshore of Flamingo. Scrawks were young birds of various kinds, curlews and herons mostly, that had left the nest but could not quite fly and spent their days flapping about inelegantly in the tops of the mangroves. If you felt inclined for some pilao or "purlo" you pulled up to the key, waded ashore, found a young bird in the top of a mangrove sapling, and shook the tree. As the bird could not fly and its hold was precarious, it tumbled down through the branches yelling *scrawk, scrawk* at the top of its avian lungs. Two would make a good mess, and that was all we ever took at a time.

As luck would have it, the first time we had gotten some scrawks we came in to Roberts' dock with our two birds lying on the thwart. As I made the painter fast, a voice came from above.

"See you got some birds for a purlo."

I looked up to see a slender, tanned face looking down at me. Just beneath the face was a large badge pinned to a white shirt. *My God*, I thought, *there's the Audubon warden, and us with two birds. Marathon jail, here we come.*

"Yeah," I drawled, "makes a change from mullet and grits."

"Nothing like a good scrawk purlo," he continued. "Just as long as you don't get to having them too often. See anything of a yacht about sixty feet long with a couple of launches towed astern?"

I shook my head.

"Tourists down from Miami," he explained. "Call themselves hunters. Real sportsmen. They got themselves some repeater shotguns and they've been running around the islands shooting the birds as they rise. They just see how many they can kill and leave the place a bloody mess."

"That's probably the shooting we heard over past Dildo Bank," Frederick told him. "We just came back from there and we saw a large boat and heard a lot of shooting."

"Thanks, boys," the warden was already jumping into his outboard boat on the other side of the dock. "I sure hope that's them. If it is, that will more than take care of those birds you got." He roared off to the northeastward.

One of the fishermen walked up. "I sure thought we were in for it with those birds," I remarked.

"Who, him?" he indicated the warden's boat in the distance.

"He won't bother anyone getting just a few birds. We got edu-
cated wardens. One tried to arrest one of us getting a few birds
for dinner and had his eyeglasses shot off his nose standing
right where I am now. Besides, they know that we take better
care of his birds than he can. No stranger's going to shoot our
birds for us."

The scrawks were cleaned, and that night we had our first Flamingo pilao, curlew cooked in rice with hot peppers and curry
powder.

There were lots of birds around the cape. Down around Lake Ingraham pink curlew or roseate spoonbills circled and wheeled
about, rosy pink against the clear blue summer sky as they came
in to roost in the dead trees on the north bank of the canal. Or
we saw them shoveling about in the mud ponds for food, using
their peculiar bills to dredge out their prey. Twice we saw wild
flamingos wading along the shore in Lake Ingraham. Flocks of
white ibis, snowy egrets, American egrets, and various herons
were common, and occasionally we would see a white pelican.
Most of the birds were little disturbed by the roar of the airboat.

Besides these birds there were numerous osprey nests and,
out on Dildo Bank, a number of eagle nests in the big dead trees.
Crocodile slides and nests were on almost every one of the offshore keys. Dildo Bank stretched away for miles to the southeast.
At high tide it could be crossed by wheel boats, but at low tide
the tops of the turtle grass were exposed along with low white
worm mounds. An airboat could skim across even wet grass, and
low water was no obstacle. When the bank dried up we often ran
in to one of the small keys. The water immediately around each
key was deep, six feet or more, and gin clear. It was a natural
aquarium filled with mullet, mangrove snapper, redfish, grouper,
grunts, and anything else that was on the bank and came to the
deeper water for refuge.

On the north bank of the Flamingo Canal past the net racks, the low cape scrub began. Wild cotton grew in the scrub, and each year trucks would arrive and government-paid wild-cotton pickers would gather the cotton and cut down the plants, all in the name of controlling the cotton boll weevil. To us fishermen, ignorant of such matters, it appeared to be a waste of money, as the closest commercially grown cotton was at least 400 miles away and unaffected by whether or not there were boll weevils at Cape Sable.

The largest tree snails in Florida lived on the stunted trees near the net racks. They were all of three inches long, cream-colored with broad bands and checkers of chocolate brown. There were also light-brown vicious scorpions. The scorpions were everywhere. At night we shook out our bedclothes before turning in. In the morning we shook out our clothes and banged our shoes on the floor to drive them out. Oddly enough, the only one that ever stung me was sitting on a net float after a set in the middle of Dildo Bank. It got me as I was hauling the net; the sting was like a heavy electric shock, but the pain was short-lived.

Summers at Flamingo were long, hot, and dry, and the ground of the wet prairie behind the village was baked hard as concrete and cracked into mosaics. Even the saltwort and sea purslane looked dead. The road from West Lake into Flamingo was marl. When it had been dragged and was dry it was like concrete. When wet it was nearly impassable, slick as grease, and soon deeply rutted by cars and the heavy fish trucks. The latter were big, eight-wheel-drive, ex-Army trucks, and they often got stuck and had to use winches mounted on their front bumpers to pull themselves down the road. The old Filimingos then used the Homestead Canal that ran parallel to the road and was kept clear for such emergencies. Today the canal is impassable even for a canoe.

The citizens of Flamingo and the officials of Monroe County had petitioned the governor to have the last part of the road paved with rock. But when the governor drove down from Miami for a look, the cavalcade roared down the hard-packed marl stretch at 60 miles an hour with hardly a bump the whole way. The cars made a quick turn around and roared back to Miami. Obviously it was one of the smoothest roads in the state, and the petition was turned down. The next day it rained and did not let up for a week. In two days the road was a bog, and nothing but the big army trucks could get through. Even those could not make it down the road to Knight's camp at Boggy Bight. The governor did not come back.

Before the rains came, a crop-duster friend of ours flew down to see us and landed on the prairie. It made a better surfaced runway than those in the tomato and bean fields he usually landed on. It was short, however. He came in on a stall but shook his head when he was ready to take off.

"It's a little short. I'll have to taxi over to the houses, rev her up, and take off over the canal."

Half of Flamingo gathered to see the take-off. The plane taxied across the flats, bumping along over the saltwort clumps, and swung around about 30 feet from the nearest house. The pilot set his brakes and began to rev up the engine. First a few bushes bent down before the backwash, then a small coconut tree blew downwards. Suddenly the back door of the house crashed in, the front door facing the bay flew open, and the air behind the house was filled with dishes, clothes, old newspapers, and even a linoleum carpet. Unaware of the debris blowing into the bay behind him, the pilot released the brakes, and the plane shot forward and leaped into the air.

When he circled back over us and wiggled his wings, the pilot was a little puzzled to see a man trying to shoot him down with a double-barreled shotgun. The irate fishermen missed the pilot but sprinkled the fuselage with buckshot. Our pilot friend felt, a little unreasonably we believed, that this was rather drastic and did not visit us again. Filimingo, by God, had won again.

When the first rains of the season came they lasted only a few minutes, but afterward the ground seemed to be moving, the surface sort of blurred. I went outside and found the ground covered with tiny frogs about half an inch long. The elder Mr. Andrews declared that they had rained down from the clouds, obviously picked up somewhere in a twister. He quoted the Bible on rains of frogs and snakes. I have never seen the phenomenon before or since and have no explanation. There were no holes in the ground from which the frogs could have emerged. They persisted for a few days and disappeared. We never saw them again.

It was shortly after this event that, one night as I lay in my camp cot, I heard a long drawn-out screaming wail in the distance. In a moment it was repeated. There was no doubt that it was the scream of a panther. I was later told by the head naturalist of the park that panthers did not scream, but they do, especially during the mating season. We saw or heard no other large animals except for an occasional deer and the ever-present raccoons.

Ellis Knight was sitting on the steps of the fish house at Boggy Bight one evening when he saw a dark shape moving slowly along the water's edge. It looked like a large ball and stopped every so often and seemed to flatten out. As it came closer, it developed into a raccoon stumbling along the shore covered by a mass of swarming mosquitoes. Ellis got the mosquito spray gun from the house and sprayed the raccoon thoroughly. The raccoon just lay there and looked at him. Ellis took a mullet out of the ice room and laid it down beside the coon. In a few minutes it picked up the fish, washed it in the water, and began to make a meal of it. Finally it went away.

The next evening the scene repeated itself, but the coon was stronger. It stopped in front of the men and was sprayed again and given another mullet. From then on it was a regular evening event for the coon to come to get sprayed and get a fish. Eventually Ellis cut a hole through the corner of the fish room large enough for the coon to reach in and get its own meal. If

Cap Knight had known that a coon was being fed on his fish, he would have driven clear to Flamingo to kill it.

The mullet fishing was not all it was cracked up to be. The big schools were late in arriving, and when they did come into the bay from their migration down the coast, they were smaller than usual and the buyers did not want them. It was the usual thing with commercial fishing. When there were no fish, the price was high. When the fish finally arrived, the price dropped so low that the fishermen made nothing. The cycle kept them in perpetual debt to the fish house.

Now, as the price fell, we heard that the fishermen over at Naples and Chokoluskee were going on strike.[7] One day the strikers' delegates showed up in Flamingo urging us to go in

Roberts' fish house, scene of the confrontation with troublemakers from Chokoloskee. (Photographer unknown, ca. 1947; courtesy of the National Park Service, Everglades National Park (EVER 15027).

with them and teach the fish houses a thing or two. Most of us were against the strike, for the truth was that the mullet *were* small and the market was glutted. As the argument got hotter we were finally told that we had to shut down Flamingo or they would shut it down for us. The strikers from up the coast were going to come over in a mob to enforce their decision.

The big day arrived, and there must have been sixty people gathered at Roberts' fish house. Mr. Roberts surveyed the crowd: "Biggest damn bunch of people ever been in Flamingo."

He looked down the dock where one of his boats had just come in. A striker yelled that they would shoot the first person who attempted to unload. Roberts walked down the dock, shouldered aside the man who had spoken, and told his fishermen to unload. They did, more worried about Roberts than about the strikers.

"You can unload it, but we'll shoot if you move it off the dock."

Roberts looked at the striker and spat in the water. "Put them in the ice house, boys, we're just getting ready to take a load into Miami." The fish were loaded into the fish house. The truck was already loaded, and ice was being added to the top layer.

"Okay, boys, finish it off with that there ice."

The whole crowd shifted and guns were brought to the fore. "You'all don't load that truck or we'll shoot you for sure," growled the spokesman. "There ain't no fish going to go out of Flamingo."

Roberts eyed him disdainfully, looked at the surly crowd that included some of his neighbors, reached behind the door, and pulled out his army rifle.

"Load her up, boys."

The ice was loaded, the heavy tarpaulin pulled over the top and lashed down.

"Okay, Buddy, let's roll." Mr. Roberts climbed into the cab, rolled the window down, and stuck the rifle out, aimed at the crowd.

"The first one of you bastards move, you'll have a bullet in your guts," and the big truck roared out of Flamingo. As it disappeared down the road, the strikers slowly walked to their cars and drove off, but not fast enough to get near the big truck or within rifle range. Filimingo, by God, had done it again.

Later Roberts remarked, "Never did have no use for those sons-a-bitches over at Chokoluskee. Don't have the guts to shoot a man unless it's dark, his back is turned, and he don't have a gun."

With the rains came the mosquitoes. I have seen them worse, but never more vicious. Old-timers who had been there working for the Model Land Company during the dredging of the canals told of black clouds of mosquitoes that surrounded the men day and night. Workmen who had to relieve themselves crouched in the water up to their waists to keep from having their tender parts bloodied by the swarms.[8]

Coming in at night with a load of fish, we stopped when we met the first mosquitoes, doused ourselves with 6–12, and tied handkerchiefs over our noses and mouths to keep out the clouds of mosquitoes. Unloading at the fish house, the fogger was kept going until the work was finished, but the nets were left in the flattie until morning when the sun was up and the mosquitoes were fewer. We kept smudges going in front of the cabin door and had to spray the cabin out before turning in, to kill the mosquitoes we had let in with us. Cracks in the floor and walls were caulked with caulking cotton. Still the pesky things would get in and buzz all night.

About this time we were driving past West Lake when Frederick stopped the car. "Look at those mullet jumping. They must weigh all of six to seven pounds."

I agreed.

"Let's bring the rig up here tomorrow and make a set."

West Lake lay immediately beside the road, and it was no

problem to launch the airboat and flattie and stow the net. We did not even go out into the lake proper but made a set in the small bayou on the edge. Those mullet were so big that if one hit you jumping the cork line it could knock you out. We worked for hours in water up to our shoulders, black as ink, and caught nine hundred pounds, all over four pounds and many going six or seven. They were so strong that it took both hands to hold one still in the boat. We took them back and weighed in at Andrews.'

"The market is just about dead," he told us, "but we'll see what they bring. West Lake may be the place to fish now."

One of the crews next to us did not wait to see the results. They took one look at those big mullet and headed for West Lake early the next morning. They came back late that night with almost no fish, worn out, and scared half to death.

"We made our set out in the lake," they told us, "and were pulling down when the net started to go under. There we were, two in the water up to our chins and one in the boat. We got out in a hurry knowing that we had something big, and be damned if we didn't have a sixteen-foot-if-he-was-an-inch, red-eyed croc rolled up in the net and mad as hell."

"Man, that croc ever hit us with his tail or get his jaws into our boat and there we would have been, sunk, a quarter of a mile from shore, and that croc after us. I tell you, fellows, you can have that West Lake and all the mullet in it."

Soon after that we set a school of mullet in Rankin Bight, only to find as we started to purse down that we had set a school of saltwater catfish. Now, catfish are just plain hell to get out of a net. They wrap the twine around their dorsal and pectoral fin spines and wriggle and kick. They are slimy, too. The only way to get them out is to shove a net cork down onto the spines and break them off. Then the webbing comes free.

It took us six hours in the sun and mosquitoes to pick all of those catfish out of the webbing. By the time we had finished,

Frederick and I had had enough of Cape Sable, mullet, red-eyed crocs, catfish, and all.

When we returned to Andrews' camp we told them we were leaving but might come back when things picked up again.

"I just got word on those West Lake mullet," he told us. "They're premium fish and they'll take all you can catch at eight to ten cents a pound."

We looked at each other, thought about the crocodiles in West Lake, and shook our heads.

The next day we stopped for a beer at the Homestead bar. There were two farmers leaning against the counter, half drunk. They eyed us as we came in. One of them straightened up and came over, swinging a beer bottle by the neck.

"Where you fellows from?" he asked.

Frederick looked him straight in the eyes.

"We're from Filimingo, by God. Want to make something of it?"

He backed away carefully. We finished our beers in peace. The next time I was in Flamingo, it was a park.

Afterword

After Frederick's get-rich-quick mullet fishing scheme fell through, Gil explored a number of options as he tried to figure out what to do with his life. For several months he worked as a bouncer at the Lakeshore Club, a fancy casino in Hypoluxo. He had determined to be a writer—a nocturnal casino job was thought to be helpful in this respect, exposing him to colorful personalities at night and freeing his afternoons for creative composition—but accumulating rejection notices from magazines were not encouraging. What to do? Walter, who had also served in the Coast Guard during the war, had returned to charterboat fishing, and Frederick soon joined him. Both appeared to be making a go of it, but college seemed like an increasingly attractive alternative. Thousands of veterans were already taking advantage of the Servicemen's Readjustment Act to go back to school.

Gil was thirty years old when he enrolled in the College of Liberal Arts at the University of Miami in June 1948. Although he had apparently never considered a scientific career before, a first-semester zoology course was transformative. Abandoning literary aspirations without regret, he threw himself headlong into biology and never looked back. His timing, in fact, was excellent.

The University of Miami had just organized a new Department of Marine Science that included curricula in fisheries, marine biology, and oceanography that had previously been offered in other departments. Closely associated with the new department was the Marine Laboratory, a semi-autonomous research unit.

Established in 1943, the laboratory had only a skeleton staff and minimal infrastructure during the war years, when it was barely sustained by small grants from the U.S. Navy. But the laboratory's director—F. G. Walton Smith, a charismatic British marine biologist—had big plans, the postwar economy was booming, and the country was now ready to spend real money on science.

As a young institution with limitless possibilities for advancement and creativity, the Marine Laboratory could not have been more welcoming to someone with Gil's background. His practical experience in commercial fisheries, his familiarity with a wide range of civilian and military marine hardware, his many connections with the sportfishing community, even his shell-collecting expertise, together provided a unique skill set that found immediate application as the marine lab began its rapid peacetime expansion. Smith's vision and enthusiasm soon attracted talented researchers and numerous students from across the country, the nucleus of future institutional greatness.[1]

Among the many students attracted to the new marine biology program at Miami was Nancy Cashman, a recent graduate from Mount Saint Agnes College in Baltimore, where she had majored in biology. Having signed up for a marine ecology course to be taught by the illustrious Professor Smith in the summer term of 1950, she was disgusted to discover, on the first day of classes, that Smith was on temporary leave from the university. Instead, the course instructor was a virtual nobody; in fact, he was a mere undergraduate teaching fellow. One thing led to another, however, and Nancy and Gil were married the following year.

Marine gamefish biology, a natural extension of Gil's prewar experience, was among his earliest research interests. In 1948 the Florida State Board of Conservation approached the Marine Laboratory with a request for information about the Atlantic sailfish, by then an economically important game species. Anglers from around the country were flocking to southeast Florida to try their skill and brawn against these hard-fighting fish, but conservation-minded sportsmen and charterboat captains were concerned about the survival of the species, of which thousands were now being caught every year. Virtually nothing was known at the time about the biology of sailfish, so a program was set up at Miami to gather relevant facts. Through his connections with the sportfishing community, Gil organized a tagging program in which fish captured by anglers were marked and released to determine whether individuals can really survive the trauma of being hooked and fought, and to find out whether the species actually migrates up and down the coast, as many charterboat-men believed. Although skeptics believed the effort was doomed to failure—a previous tagging program in the Gulf of California had failed spectacularly—the Miami project scored its first suc-cess when a fish captured and tagged off Stuart on January 28, 1951, was caught off Palm Beach on March 15. Additional recap-tures in the months that followed showed that at least some fish do survive to fight again, and that individual fish do not travel very far, suggesting that the species is not migratory.

This research program also involved examining the stomach contents of sailfish and other species that were brought back to the docks. With the enthusiastic cooperation of fishermen and taxidermists up and down the coast, hundreds of stomachs were examined. Most of the items found in sailfish stomachs were fish, but a surprising fraction—almost 20 percent—were cepha-lopods (octopods and squid). Interestingly, at least some of the fishes found in sailfish stomachs were bottom-dwelling species. Although sailfish were previously thought to be surface feeders, these results suggested that they sometimes dive deep to feed.

Gil's sailfish work soon attracted the attention of the Na-tional Geographic Society, which was then a major source of scientific research funding. One of the least well understood as-pects of sailfish biology was reproduction. Gil knew that sailfish

Gil opening a dolphin to collect stomach contents as renowned fish taxidermist Al Pflueger looks on. Photo by B. Anthony Stewart, 1954; National Geographic Creative.

spawned inshore—between the beach and the reef—where, as a charterboat captain, he had repeatedly caught adult females with ripe eggs. But where were the young sailfish? Nothing that looked like hatchling sailfish had ever been found near the beach or over the reef.

Some marine fishes were already known to spend their early life in the plankton, the living soup of almost-microscopic plants and animals that float near the surface in the open ocean. With support from the National Geographic Society, the marine lab began to sample the plankton by trawling the surface of the Gulf Stream between Florida and the Bahamas, using fine silk nets at night. For the lab's researchers, this plankton fishing was every bit as thrilling as fighting the adult fish was for sportsmen.

At the run's end we cut the throttle and hauled in the net. Gently we lifted over the side the glass jar at its end. Under the cabin light we saw innumerable forms dart about the container of sea water—arrowworms, comb jellies, siphonophores, medusae, and the transparent larvae, or very young, of fish.

There at the bottom, just as we were about to add the preservatives and store the haul away, three tiny creatures caught our attention. They were fish we had never seen before—steel blue in places, transparent elsewhere, with short, broad snouts and toothed spines projecting from their heads.

They bore no resemblance to the lean greyhounds of the sea we all knew so well, yet they closely fitted the tentative description of infant sailfish made years ago by the famed Danish ichthyologist, Christian F. Lütken.

Excitement soared. Were we at last on the track of sailfish young?[2]

They were, and they were also capturing the hitherto unknown larval forms of many other fish species. Unraveling the life secrets of fish with planktonic larvae was painstaking work that involved sorting through tens of thousands of minute specimens and making thousands of detailed drawings, tasks that occupied Nancy Voss and other project personnel for several years. The results, however, convincingly tied the life of the Gulf Stream to the ecology of inshore waters, and vice versa, an important early lesson for marine conservationists.

Another early research interest was cephalopods, a group that offered far greater scope for original discoveries than fish. Ichthyology—the scientific study of fishes—was already a mature research field in the late 1940s, and the shallow-water fish fauna

Nancy Voss (née Cashman) drawing planktonic fish larvae as part of the marine laboratory's research program on gamefish biology. Photo by B. Anthony Stewart, 1954; National Geographic Creative.

of the western Atlantic was reasonably well known. By contrast, undiscovered and unnamed cephalopods still lurked near at hand in the marine habitats of south Florida. Even a beginner could make significant discoveries.

As an undergraduate I once found an octopus sunning itself in a submerged grassy spot in Lake Worth, Florida. With some hesitation I dived in and seized it. The creature's eight arms and hundreds of suckers wrapped around my wrist. After maneuvering it into a jar, I studied my prize. A small animal, it had a body hardly larger than my thumb, but each arm was more than a foot long. I marveled at the play of colors over the mantle, rippling hues that outdid the performance of any chameleon.

No book was able to help me identify my catch, and two specialists couldn't name it. Twenty years after its capture I finally found its twin in the Royal Institute of Natural Science in Brussels, Belgium. It was *Octopus defilippi*, previously known only from the Mediterranean Sea and the west coast of Africa. The very first octopus I had ever captured proved to be the first of its species identified from the western Atlantic![3]

Equally important to a young scientist at the outset of his research career, hardly anyone was working on cephalopod taxonomy in the early postwar years, so there was lots of academic elbow room.

Cephalopods are mollusks, a group with which Gil was already intimately familiar from his shell-collecting youth, but they differ strikingly from other mollusks in many ways. Whereas most mollusks have hard external shells, most cephalopods do not. Also, most other mollusks are sessile (remaining attached to one spot, like oysters and mussels), burrow in soft sand or mud (like clams), or crawl slowly along the bottom (like conchs and whelks), but cephalopods are fast, agile swimmers. Many mollusks are filter feeders or grazers with only the simplest kinds of reflexive behavior, but most cephalopods are active predators, some of which exhibit remarkably complex behaviors. And a few, like the common octopus, appear to be capable of observational learning and tool use.

Cephalopods are also astonishingly diverse, ranging in size from the very small to the very large, and they live at all depths throughout the world oceans. One of the smallest is the pygmy squid (*Pickfordiateuthis pulchella*). Less than two inches long, it was first discovered lurking in shallow-water grass beds near Miami by collectors from the Marine Laboratory; Gil named it as a new genus and species in 1953. By contrast, the giant squid (*Architeuthis dux*), perhaps reaching 60 feet or more in total length, is a deep-sea creature rarely seen at the surface. In appearance, cephalopods range from the vaguely sinister—the so-called vampire squid (*Vampyroteuthis infernalis*) is cloaked in black webbing—to the exceptionally beautiful. Among the loveliest is the blue-ringed octopus of Australia, and some midwater squid are extravagantly bejeweled with flashing light organs.

Among Gil's earliest research articles, published while he was still an undergraduate, were descriptions of several new species of octopus and squid, all discovered within a few miles of Miami. Describing new species was painstaking work that involved considerable bibliographic research and careful comparisons with previously collected specimens. At that time, long before the scientific literature was digitized and readily accessible online, taxonomic researchers needed first-hand access to rare books and to copies of articles published in obscure scientific periodicals. Taxonomic research also required collection facilities: a safe place to store and organize specimens for scientific study. Book by book and reprint by reprint, Gil accumulated the necessary research library for taxonomic research on cephalopods, and he soon became the first curator of the Marine Laboratory's invertebrate museum.

Cephalopod taxonomy was the topic of Gil's Masters and PhD theses, and it would remain a central research theme for the rest of his life, bringing him international recognition. Although his earliest work was on the octopus and squid of Florida coastal waters, the Caribbean, and the Gulf of Mexico, later publications described the cephalopod faunas of the Philippines, South Africa, the northeastern Pacific, and elsewhere. He also trained a new generation of cephalopod researchers, and many of his students went on to have long and productive academic careers of their own.[4]

Gil was an early and influential advocate of cephalopod fisheries. For centuries before fried calamari and grilled octopus became popular among American foodies, cephalopods were important items in the diets of many Asian and southern European

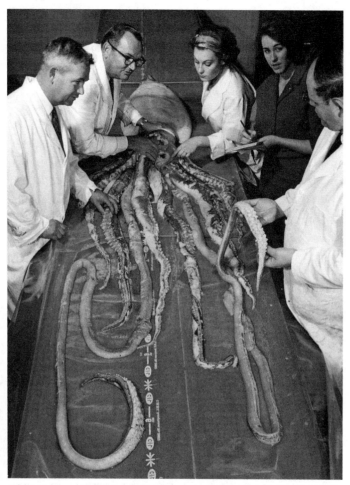

Gil (*second from left*) helping to dissect a young female giant squid at St. John's, Newfoundland. Photo by Robert Sisson, 1965; National Geographic Creative.

cultures. Gil was keenly interested in the traditional methods used by Old World artisanal fisheries for octopus and squid, and he drew attention to opportunities for commercial harvesting of cephalopods in regions where traditional fisheries did not exist. He also advocated research to ensure that cephalopod stocks were not overexploited by industrial-scale fisheries operations.

Popular articles on squid and octopus written for the *National Geographic Magazine* and *Sea Frontiers* helped communicate his enthusiasm for studying and eating cephalopods.[5]

As the Marine Laboratory acquired larger and larger research vessels in the 1950s and 1960s, it became possible to conduct oceanographic research farther and farther from Miami and to explore ever-deeper reaches of the tropical Atlantic. The 78-foot GERDA—a former yacht with a sturdy North Sea trawler hull, fitted out for oceanographic work in 1955—was used for biological surveys in the Straits of Florida and the Bahamas, where laboratory staff gained much useful experience with a variety of sampling gear and obtained scientifically valuable collections. The accumulating research results from the GERDA cruises, however, suggested the need to extend survey work throughout the tropical Atlantic, including the West Indies, the north coast of South America, and the west coast of Africa. When the laboratory finally acquired a vessel large enough for months-long cruises and sufficiently powerful to tow deep-sea sampling gear, Gil and his colleagues were ready.

The 173-foot JOHN ELLIOT PILLSBURY, originally designed and built for troop supply in World War II, was modified and outfitted for marine research in 1963. Supported by grants from the National Science Foundation and the National Geographic Society, she made a historic series of collecting expeditions from 1964 to 1969 focused on the deep-sea fauna of the tropical Atlantic. Gil directed this program from its outset, and he was chief scientist on many cruises, notably including those in West African and Panamanian waters. He was also chief scientist aboard the cruise that first trawled the bottom of the Puerto Rico Trench, the deepest part of the North Atlantic Ocean.

The PILLSBURY's normal complement included twenty-two crew members and fourteen scientists, she had multiple laboratory facilities and custom-built sampling gear designed to reach ocean depths previously inaccessible to biologists, and she operated for months at a time thousands of miles from her home port. The staffing, logistics, and equipping of these expeditions were complex problems, and the costs were correspondingly formidable. In today's scientific funding environment, such an ambitious biological survey program would be unthinkable, but science was more generously supported in the 1960s and, very fortunately, institutions and individuals seized the day and made the most of their unique opportunities.

The PILLSBURY's two cruises to the Gulf of Guinea in West Africa included an all-star cast of senior marine biologists, notably Frederick M. Bayer, a cnidarian specialist from Miami; Lipke B. Holthuis, the renowned crustacean authority from Leiden; and the ichthyologist C. Richard Robins, also from Miami. Gil's published logs of the PILLSBURY's West African cruises tell what it was like to be chief scientist, where his seamanship and expert knowledge of marine hardware were huge assets.

> May 16th, Sunday [1965]
>
> The rest of the day was one of those that drives one to drink but then suddenly changes and ends perfectly. The trouble began at 1120 when we shot the 40-foot trawl in 2441 meters. I decided to fish it . . . at 2 knots with a 40° wire angle and 5000 m.w.o. [meters of wire out]. We paid out at a rate of 80 m.p.m. [meters per minute] with both engines at 400 r.p.m. All went well until we had run out 2690 meters of wire when Dave, who was operating the winch, reported a frayed strand and stopped the winch. I went below . . . and found that . . . trawl and wire were hanging by only two strands. We reduced power to one engine to slow the ship and heaved in until the wire break was between the traction drums and the storage drum. Then we stopped off the wire with two come-alongs on

deck, and pulled the bight of the wire on deck to the rigging bench where the bos'n and Bob, the ordinary seaman, cut it and put in a double short splice, laying each end past the other as in an eye splice. . . . We then continued paying out but at 1435, with 3226 meters out, a bad straightened kink in the half-inch wire appeared. The same splicing procedure had to be repeated. . . . Again we paid out. When 5000 meters was reached we held for half an hour to see if contact with the bottom was made by a change in the tensionometer. It held steady at 1500 pounds! . . . We decided the tensionometer was not working properly and paid out to 6500 meters and commenced trawling.

At this point I left the forecastle head to do some typing in my cabin when I heard over the intercom the words "hung up" and "Voss." I made record time to the winch. The ship had been stopped and swung around by the wire. I immediately took all way off the ship and started hauling in. There was a heavy strain so I had the mate put the rudder hard down to starboard and come ahead on the port engine. This swung us around and got the wire leading forward. I then had him hold on that heading for a couple of minutes and then again took the way off of her. This did the trick and we hauled in with no difficulty. . . .

We got the shackle up at 2120 and had the net on deck at 2132. . . . The catch was very good. . . . Among the crustaceans were a *Willemoesia*, a new species of *Notostomus*, *Polycheles*, *Plesiopenaeus*, *Eryoneicus*, numerous bivalves, anemones, a *Vampyroteuthis*, and a number of white-bodied slender fishes of the family Scopelarchidae which Dick Robins says are new to our cruises. So all the work was not in vain![6]

In all the salt waters adjoining the continental United States, coral reefs are found only in Florida, where they extend in a long arc from Fowey Rock, just south of Miami, to the Dry Tortugas, about 65 miles west of Key West. More than fifty coral species are found in this archipelago of barrier and patch reefs, including over three-quarters of all the species of reef-building corals known to occur in the tropical Atlantic. The largest and most luxuriantly developed of Florida's coral reefs, and the most vulnerable to human encroachment, are those that occur off north Key Largo.

The Key Largo reefs are special places. On a sunlit day, back when the reef was healthy and the water was "gin clear," your gently rocking boat seemed to be magically suspended above golden groves of branching corals that swarmed with brightly colored fish. Sea fans, sea whips, and anemones anchored to the coral waved back and forth, keeping slow tempo with the surge of ocean waves. Loggerhead turtles foraged above the reef, barracudas menacingly patrolled its margins, and porpoises sported nearby. A diver could find abundant spiny lobsters lurking in deep crevices under the corals, as wary reef squid hovered overhead. Close inspection would reveal a rich tapestry of invertebrate life on the corals themselves: encrusting sponges and bryozoans, busy cleaner shrimp, long-spined sea urchins, feather worms, and myriad other species. A fringe of clean white bottom surrounded the reef, extending outward only as far as grazing reef fishes dared to venture for fear of predators. Beyond, shoreward, lay vast beds of turtle grass, productive nurseries of many ecologically important reef species and a vital part of the keys' marine ecosystem, which extends from the mangrove-fringed coastline to the very edge of the continental shelf.

Until the end of World War II these reefs were essentially pristine, visited only by lobster fishermen or the occasional— and therefore harmless—amateur shell collector. Shipping traditionally gave the reefs a wide berth. For hundreds of years sailing vessels had come to grief on the corals, first grounded and then beaten to pieces in storms by the pounding surf. Although shipwrecks did some damage, this was soon repaired by the coral animals themselves: tiny polyps that built the stony fabric of the reef inch by inch over the long years while they remained unpolluted and mostly undisturbed by man.

Gil knew the Key Largo reefs well, having visited them as a young shell collector and later, just after the war, on numerous research field trips to the upper keys. The local invertebrate life was also familiar from his close study of the shallow-water fauna of nearby Soldier Key, where he and Nancy completed an intensive biological survey in 1955. In effect, Gil knew what the reefs once looked like—what they were *supposed* to look like—and more to the point, he was in a position to speak with authority about them when they needed protection. That time was soon at hand.

The first serious damage to Florida's coral reefs came from postwar treasure hunters who began dynamiting parts of the outer reef and using suction dredges to excavate wrecks. Commercial collecting soon became an important problem too. As newly affluent, automobile-owning tourists flooded into south Florida, hundreds of curio stores sprang up along U.S. 1 from the Palm Beaches to Key West, each with roadside piles of bleached coral fragments and conch shells to lure customers inside. Hordes of workmen flocked to the reefs with hammers, grapples, and crowbars to supply the curio stores with their stock in trade. At about the same time, a thriving business sprang up to provide tropical fish hobbyists with colorful reef species. Spearfishing, a newly popular sport, added to the toll of reef degradation and destruction. The Key Largo reefs, close to the mainland and easily accessed from major population centers, suffered the most from this unwelcome attention.

Some conservationists were already aware of the biological importance and vulnerability of the Key Largo reef system. In fact, protecting this unique marine habitat was part of the original proposal for the Everglades National Park, the hypothetical eastern boundary of which once extended all the way across Key Largo to include the barrier reefs. When this plan became public knowledge, however, the howls of protest could be heard all the way to Washington. The loudest objections, and the hardest to ignore politically, came from wealthy Key Largo landowners and from the Monroe County government at Key West, which was alarmed that so much land might be lost from its tax rolls. To save the park proposal from such determined opposition, the eastern boundary was redrawn in 1946 to exclude Key Largo and its coral reefs.

In the decade that followed the establishment of the Everglades National Park, conditions on the reefs deteriorated seriously, but the situation was not widely recognized as dire. Something clearly had to be done, but what? The opportunity for effective action arrived in June 1957, when a meeting of scientists and forestry researchers was convened to discuss the future development of the park. Gil attended this meeting as an official representative of the Marine Laboratory, tasked with reporting on the need for basic research on the park's marine ecosystems. On the last day of the meeting, report duly delivered, he asked if he could now speak as a private individual about a problem outside the park's boundary but of major importance to those attending the meeting. Permission granted, he described an appalling state of affairs.

The preceding weekend over 50 boats had been counted on Key Largo Dry Rocks and adjacent reefs loading coral, including a barge with a big crane for hoisting aboard whole massive pieces. When seen, its deck was already heaped high with corals. The same weekend treasure hunters were dynamiting part of Long Reef in search of wreck remains. On one reef several boats were anchored with their crews collecting tropical fish, forming a line across the reef and overturning every turnable rock or coral slab to scare the small fish out into the open. It was obvious that with this kind of activity increasing weekly there would soon be no corals left.[7]

He told the meeting that something must be done, and soon, to protect the reefs, and that the area should be made a park.

An expert had spoken, and the meeting was galvanized to action. A chart of the upper keys was produced, and the boundaries of the hypothetical park were marked out. To avoid political opposition from property owners and the Monroe County government, no land was included in the proposed park. A motion to petition the Department of the Interior and the National Park Service to preserve this area was passed unanimously, and telegrams were sent to the governor and the secretary of the interior before the meeting was adjourned.

The notion of an undersea park was a new one. None then existed in the United States, and the sheer novelty of creating a submarine preserve was appealing to many interested parties, but there were novel obstacles too. Action by both the state and federal governments was needed. The state had jurisdiction from the land to three miles offshore, but three miles was not enough to include most of the barrier reef. The waters beyond the three-mile limit were under federal control. Political coordination as well as a massive public relations effort were needed to make the park a reality.

John Pennekamp, associate editor of the *Miami Herald*, played a key role in the ensuing public relations campaign. Well known in Washington (where he had recently won an important Supreme Court case concerning freedom of the press) and a member of the Florida Board of Parks and Historic Memorials, he was also effective politically, and many other influential people were soon involved in the marathon effort to sway legislators and administrations in Tallahassee and Washington over the next several years. Remarkably, however, only light resistance was encountered, necessary state and federal action was taken, and the Pennekamp Coral Reef State Park was dedicated on December 10, 1960. Unfortunately, the real fight to save the reefs had only just begun.

Threats to the Key Largo reef system and other nearby marine habitats continued to multiply as south Florida's postwar population increased unsustainably, decade after decade. Among others, an oil refinery and plastics factory were proposed to be built on the adjacent mainland and supplied by a tanker channel dredged straight across the reef. Next, Florida Power and Light proposed to dump superheated water from its new nuclear reactors directly into Biscayne Bay. Additionally, dredge-and-fill operations up and down the keys churned up bottom sediments and increased water turbidity over the reefs, and mushrooming keys developments dumped increasing quantities of untreated sewage at sea. Gil repeatedly testified as expert witness at numerous public hearings and in many court cases as conservationists and other concerned citizen groups tried to stop these environmentally irresponsible activities, and in many cases they were successful in doing so.

Gil's testimony was often effective because he knew what he was talking about and because he had the relevant facts and figures at his fingertips. He also expressed himself vigorously and did not mince words. When he was on one side of an issue there was no doubt about it, and he was hard to ignore.

"He always has the marvelous appearance of somebody who has dived a thousand, million times," says long-time environmental activist Dagney Johnson, who is now president of the Upper Keys Citizens Association. "You just know this man has been out on sloops, on schooners, on every kind of boat you can think of. He makes a telling speech. He's very dignified, very much to the point and unrelenting in his stating of the scientific facts, while expressing real emotional commitment to the health of the reef and convincing regret at its decline.

"Everybody is always coming down here telling us what to do, and that is not what Gil does," says Johnson. "He comes down here to tell us how it is."[8]

It became a lifelong commitment. Much of Gil's professional career from 1960 onward was focused on environmental issues related to coral reefs, even as he continued to work on cephalopod taxonomy and directed the Marine Laboratory's wide-ranging deep-sea program. At the outset, a major problem was the lack of reliable information about local coral reef ecology. Marine Laboratory researchers played a major role in remedying the situation, with pioneering surveys of coral reef fish diversity by Walter A. Starck, experimental studies of patch-reef community dynamics by Gil and Frederick M. Bayer, and studies of reef-fish feeding habits by C. Richard Robins. A large environmental assessment of the Key Largo reefs that Gil undertook in the early 1980s provided an essential baseline for tracking future changes in the ecosystem, and just before he died in 1989 he was awarded a major grant to study the effects of pollution on the coral reefs of the upper keys. In recognition of his decades-long efforts, a 1988 *Miami Herald* article styled him "Keeper of the Reefs," an apt title that might well have served as Gil's epitaph had he needed a headstone. Soon afterward, we laid him to rest in the Gulf Stream.

The struggle to save the reefs continues, and final victory is by no means sure. For reasons that are still unclear, coral reefs are in decline across the Caribbean and around the world. Global decline suggests that global factors are at least partially responsible, but regional threats are obviously important too, and local conservation efforts are still needed if these ancient and ecologically vital habitats are to be preserved for future generations. Although he cannot be said to have won the fight for Florida's coral reefs, it is not the least of Gil's accomplishments that, on his watch when so much was at stake, he did not lose it.

Acknowledgments

In preparing Dad's manuscript for publication I had crucial help from family, friends, and colleagues. My mother, Nancy Voss, scoured old files and bookshelves in Miami for anything relevant to this project; my aunt, Marjorie Nelson, contributed photographs, obscure references, manuscripts, and many otherwise unremembered details of family history; and my cousin Harvey Oyer III provided scans of several old family photographs, including the iconic 1886 portrait of Lake Worth pioneers. My sister, Linda Voss, produced the first electronic version of Dad's text in 1992 using now-extinct word processing software; fortunately, the surviving hard copy was machine-readable decades later.

I am grateful to Tad Bennicoff of the Smithsonian Institution Archives, who ferreted out Hannibal Pierce's correspondence with Spencer F. Baird, and to the experienced personnel at the United States National Archives, who helped me locate the original log books of CG 41009 and CG 42028. My research on prewar Florida fisheries and other relevant topics would not have been possible without access to a world-class natural history library, for which I thank Tom Baione and his diligent staff at the American Museum of Natural History (AMNH). Matthew Shanley of the AMNH Photo Studio scanned several old photographs for this book; Ashley Morton of National Geographic Creative granted permission to reproduce images that first appeared in Dad's *National Geographic* articles; and Bonnie

Ciolino, archivist at the South Florida Collections Management Center, Everglades National Park, was instrumental in locating pictures of old Flamingo. Patricia J. Wynne, good friend and long-time colleague, took a special interest in this project and drew the two maps that grace this volume in characteristically elegant detail.

The family is grateful to the late Donald P. de Sylva, an authority on southeastern coastal fisheries and marine fish biology, for reading Dad's original text in 1990 and encouraging us to publish it. Subsequent efforts to interest local presses in the manuscript were unsuccessful, however, so it was set aside for many years as we all got on with our lives. Sian Hunter, acquisitions editor at the University Press of Florida, subsequently read Dad's stories and suggested that bracketing biographical material be written to put them in context; her enthusiasm and support were important throughout the final stages of manuscript preparation and revision. Last, I thank my wife, Nancy Simmons, and youngest son, Matthew, for their consistent good humor and patience with a project that consumed far too much of my attention at home for many months.

Glossary

Life afloat involves many actions, objects, and concepts unfamiliar to those who live ashore, so vocabulary that Gil used unselfconsciously may be incomprehensible to some readers. The following definitions are mostly consistent with standard usage in nautical dictionaries (e.g., Kemp 1976) or with prevailing usage in southeastern fisheries (Siebenaler 1955). Asterisks indicate words that are defined elsewhere in the glossary.

Aft. At or toward the *stern of a boat or ship; the usual adjectival form is "after," as in the after cabin (the sternmost of two or more cabins).

Aloft. Overhead; typically used as the destination or position of someone who has climbed the *standing rigging to the yards, *crosstrees, or upper masts of a ship.

Astern. A position behind the *stern of a vessel, or a stern-ward direction of travel or motion.

Backstay. Part of the *standing rigging of a sailing vessel, backstays are stout ropes that (together with the forestays) provide fore-and-aft support to the masts. In general, backstays are named for mast they support; the main backstay, for example, supports the main mast.

Bilges. The lowest spaces inside the hull of a ship, one on either side of the keel, where water tends to collect and which must periodically be pumped dry.

Bos'n (also bo'sun or bosun). The phonetic spelling for

"boatswain's mate" as pronounced by seamen; the officer in charge of the ship's hull, rigging, anchors, cables, et cetera.

Box garboard. Apparently (I can find no explicit definition), a flat extension of the keel formed by the garboard strakes (the lowermost planks of the hull), which allows a beached boat to stand upright.

Bow. The fore-most end of a vessel, the opposite end from the *stern.

Broach. To turn broadside to, and therefore to lose control in, following seas, such that the vessel is at the mercy of oncoming waves.

Bulwark. The planking along the sides of a ship that prevents seas from washing over the deck or sailors from getting washed overboard in rough weather.

Bunt. The slack belly of a sail; a good thing to land in if you are so unfortunate as to slip and fall while *aloft.

Chandlery. A store specializing in marine supplies, with which seamen usually had lines of credit, and from which they were sometimes contractually obliged to buy necessary items.

Chocks. Wooden cradles used to hold a ship's boats on deck.

Coaming. A raised lip that frames the opening of a hatchway, designed to prevent water on the deck from spilling into the *hold.

Cork line. The head rope of a gill net or seine, strung with floats (traditionally corks) to keep the net vertically oriented in the water.

Counter. The arch forming the overhanging *stern of a vessel above the waterline.

Crosstrees. Wooden spreaders fixed at the upper ends of the lower masts to support and spread the topmast *shrouds. A place to sit while *aloft and scanning the horizon for other ships.

Cuddy. A small cabin.

Davits. Small cranes fitted with hoisting and lowering gear

from which a ship's boats can be lowered over the sides or
*stern.

Dinghy. A small open (undecked) boat usually propelled by
oars.

Fathom. An ancient unit of measurement, originally based
on the distance between a man's outstretched arms,
standardized under the old imperial system to be equivalent
to six feet. Fathoms were normally used by mariners to
express water depth ("Full fathom five thy father lies; of his
bones are coral made . . ." etc.) but sometimes also for the
lengths of cables and other ropes. On hydrographic charts,
and in traditional maritime usage, depths of less than five
fathoms were customarily expressed in feet.

Fender. Any cushioning object let down over the side to
prevent chafing between two vessels or between a vessel and
a dock or wharf. Historically fenders were woven from rope,
but nowadays they are usually rubber or plastic.

Flattie. A small, straight-sided, flat-bottomed, *sloop-rigged
working boat peculiar to the Chesapeake and other shallow
southern waters.

Flying bridge. On small fishing craft, an open deck provided
with secondary navigational controls located above the
pilothouse or main cabin.

Fo'c'sle (from "forecastle"). The space immediately beneath
the forward deck of a sailing vessel, often used as sleeping
quarters for the crew.

Forecastle head. The forward part of the forecastle deck. On
the PILLSBURY the winch controls were on the after rail on
the starboard side of the forecastle head.

Forepeak. The forward-most section of the hold of a ship,
formed by the angle of the *bow and often used for stowage.

Gaff-headed. Referring to a fore-and-aft sail, the top edge of
which is laced to a spar (or gaff) fitted to the after side of a
mast.

Gill. To be caught behind the gill covers in the *mesh of a gill net; fish that have become entangled in this way are said to have gilled.

Grapnel. A small four-pronged anchor often used as such by small craft but sometimes also used as a grappling hook.

Gunwales (pronounced "gunnels"). In these narratives, the upper edge of the sides of a boat, essentially equivalent to the rail of a ship.

Hanging-in. The process of attaching net *webbing to a *cork line and a *lead line, accomplished with a net needle and twine.

Hard-laid. Describing line or rope made of tightly twisted strands, making it both less likely to tangle and less apt to absorb water than soft-laid line or rope (with less tightly twisted strands).

Head. The seat of ease (toilet), often lacking on small working vessels.

Hold. The below-deck compartment or compartments used for storage (usually of ice and/or fish in these narratives), accessed by large square hatches on the deck.

Hove-to. Brought as nearly to a standstill as can be accomplished at sea; said of a sailing vessel brought up into the wind with her sails shortened and trimmed such that no headway is made.

Jigger (or jigger-mast). A small mast set right aft (e.g., on the *taffrail) to carry a small sail, also known as a jigger.

Lapstreak. A method of hull construction in which the lower margin of each row (or strake) of planks overlaps the upper margin of the row beneath it; also spelled "lapstrake." The equivalent British term is "clinker-built."

Lazarette. Below-deck compartment for the stowage of items in the stern of a ship. Thus, to search a ship from *forepeak to lazarette is to search her *hold from one end to another.

Lead line. The foot rope of a gill net or seine, strung with weights (traditionally lead sinkers) to keep the bottom of the net submerged.

Lee. Referring to the side of the ship away from the wind (i.e., the side that does not have the wind blowing on it), opposite of *weather.

Mesh. The holes in the *webbing formed by the twine from which a net is woven.

Outriggers. Long poles mounted on the sides of sportfishing boats that allow multiple lines to be trolled without becoming entangled. Back in the day, trolled lines were attached to the outriggers with clothespins that would snap free when a fish struck the bait.

Painter. A length of rope, usually attached to a ringbolt in the bow, by which a small boat is secured to a pier, dock, jetty, or ship.

Purse seine. A net towed at the surface by one or more boats to capture schooling fish. Like beach seines (described in the text), purse seines have a *cork line and a *lead line to keep the *webbing vertically oriented in the water. The schooling fish are first encircled and the net is then "pursed" (closed at the bottom by pulling on a line threaded through rings on the lead line) to prevent the fish from escaping. Boats engaged in purse seining were known as purse boats.

Rail. The upper edge of the *bulwark, over which one leans or fishes, as the case may be. On a wooden sailing vessel the cap rail was the uppermost trim on the rail, i.e., the surface on which one might have slipped while inexpertly boarding her over the bulwark, or which might have been grooved by friction with hand lines over years of fishing.

Ratlines (pronounced "ratlins"). The rope steps by which the *shrouds are climbed to go *aloft.

Schooner. The usual term for vessels with two or more masts rigged with fore-and-aft sails, but often used in a restricted sense for those with two masts only, of which the mainmast is taller than the foremast.

Scuppers. Holes pierced through the bulwarks at deck level to allow water on the deck to drain over the sides of the ship.

Shrouds. Part of the *standing rigging, the shrouds are stout ropes that provide lateral support to the masts. Like stays, shrouds are named for the masts they support, thus main shrouds, et cetera.

Sloop. A single-masted, fore-and-aft rigged sailing vessel; thus, a boat with one mast and fore-and-aft sails is said to be sloop-rigged.

Smack. Among Gulf Coast fishermen, a synonym for *schooner. Amateur etymologists have speculated that the word locally derives from the slapping sound of water in the live wells of early snapper schooners, but as "smack" is widely used elsewhere as a generic term for small fishing vessels, no local derivation seems necessary.

Squat boards. Flat boards attached to the *transom of a motorized boat above the propeller(s) and parallel to the water's surface, designed to keep the stern from "squatting" (a hydrodynamic sinking effect) under power.

Standing rigging. The fixed, permanent rigging of a sailing vessel; on small *schooners the standing rigging consists primarily of the heavy ropes (stays and *shrouds) that support the masts.

Stern. The back (or after) end of a ship or boat, the opposite end from the *bow.

Taffrail. The after *rail on the *stern of a ship.

Thwart. A transverse plank on which to sit in an open (undecked) boat, such as a *dinghy or *flattie.

Tiller. A bar of wood or metal fitted into or onto the head of the rudder, traditionally used for steering before the widespread adoption of steering wheels on larger vessels. On small motorized craft with steering wheel and engine controls forward, a removable tiller can be shipped to transfer control of the rudder to someone in the stern and to provide more leverage for steering in heavy seas.

Trammel net. A fishing net consisting of three layers (or walls) of *webbing attached to a single *cork line and *lead line. The outer walls are made of very large-meshed webbing, whereas the inner wall is smaller-meshed. "Fish are captured by passing between the large meshes of the outer wall, then pushing the small-mesh inner wall into a pocket between the large meshes of the wall on the opposite side of the net" (Siebenaler 1955: 20).

Transom. The flat *stern of a flat-sterned boat or ship.

Trawl. A large bag-shaped net, usually towed along the bottom or at other subsurface depths, to capture fish, shrimp, or other marine organisms. The mouth of a towed trawl can be held open by "doors" (boards provided with bridles that hold them at an outward angle, one on each side of the net), depressor vanes, stiff frames, hoops, or other devices, and the catch is collected at the narrow ("cod") end.

Waist. That part of the upper deck of a ship between the mainmast and the foremast.

Weather. Referring to the side or deck (of a ship) exposed to the elements; thus, the weather side is that facing the wind (i.e., the side on which the wind is blowing); opposite of *lee. Handline fishing was always done from the weather *rail, so that the boat did not drift over the lines.

Webbing. The fabric of a net, woven of twine to form *mesh of a size appropriate for the species of fish to be caught.

Notes

Foreword

1. To the best of my knowledge, the only surviving letter written by H. D. Pierce is preserved among the papers of Spencer Fullerton Baird, who headed the United States Fish Commission from 1871 to 1887 and also served as the second secretary of the Smithsonian Institution (where his correspondence is now archived). Hannibal's letter of October 13, 1883, is gracefully written in a firm cursive script, without blotting or corrections. Fluently composed, grammatically correct, and confident in tone, it suggests a careful early education, wide reading, and many years of epistolary experience. Interestingly, his letters to Baird (of which only the one survives) contained original observations about the migratory movements of fish as well as closely reasoned arguments concerning the causes of occasional fish kills on the east coast of Florida. Baird thought these observations and inferences important enough that they were promptly published, with appropriate attribution, in the *Bulletin of the United States Fish Commission* (H. D. Pierce 1884). A sample paragraph conveys an interesting impression of the man:

> In regard to my theory that it was cold water that killed the fish, I did not mean in the Gulf of Mexico, but on the Atlantic seaboard of Florida, where I have seen it happen several times, but I have no doubt it is the same in the Gulf. I think that I ought to be a pretty good judge of cold water, as when a boy I took many a swim in the ice-laden streams of Maine, and later in life many an involuntary plunge into the waters of the Arctic Ocean to get out of the way of the flukes of the bow-head whale; and I must say that I never was so thoroughly chilled as on that afternoon in July on the coast of Florida. On that occasion, while disrobed, I saw two or three fish floating about, just alive. . . . The next day, upon going to the beach, there were thousands of them

ashore, and many floating helplessly about on the surface of the water. . . . The only reason or cause I can give, and I do not know as it will hold good, is that the Gulf Stream, in its rush northward, must have a counter-current inshore, running south. If the stream can force the warm water of the tropics from the equator to 50° or 55° north latitude, why may not the counter-current bring to Florida occasionally a body of water cold enough to kill fish such as live in the tropics?

2. Riviera and Boynton later added "Beach" to their names, doubtless to sound more attractive as they competed for northern settlers. West Palm Beach was built by Flagler to house the workers for his oceanside resort hotels, so its suffix was original.

3. Margaret Garnett was the daughter of Andrew Garnett, another local pioneer. Her memoirs (Harris 1990) include a brief description of the Voss household in the early 1900s and a useful map of the landholdings between the railroad and lakeshore at Hypoluxo, where the Garnetts, Porters, and Vosses lived.

4. A substantial extract from Uncle Charlie's voluminous manuscript was published by the University of Miami Press as *Pioneer Life in Southeast Florida* (C. W. Pierce 1970). Much of the historical content in this foreword is drawn from that manuscript, from Grandmother's unpublished diary, and from other family papers, family oral tradition, and Voss (1968).

5. The logs Gil kept of these early voyages are examples of a lifelong penchant for nautical record keeping, a useful skill that would carry over into his professional life as coastguardsman and scientist:

Monday, June 22 [1936]
Had an early breakfast and got underway with light south wind and weather tide. No rain all day. Noon off Sands Key. About dark just inside Caesar's Creek we passed the sponging fleet. Got into the Hawk Channel on the turn of the tide and ran down Key Largo several miles before anchoring near shore in five feet of water. Can hear mosquitoes on shore. Looks squally.

Tuesday, June 23
Plenty of mosquitoes during the night. Towards morning had bad squall from southeast. Boat rolled and pitched badly. . . . Started down Hawk Channel with heavy easterly gale under all sail. Heavy seas in the channel. Sharpie rode them like a duck.

In about twenty minutes lowered mainsail and scudded along under foresail. Gale moderated and hoisted reefed mainsail. . . . 10:00 anchored in lee of Sand Point and made coffee and pancakes. Rode out another heavy squall. . . . Left Sand Point at 11:00 under reefed mainsail and full foresail and riding through the combers squared away for the Dreggers. Successive heavy squalls, wind and rain, channel rough. Had to lay bow to wind in some squalls and let the sails shake. Channel full of big combers. Made it to lee of the Dreggers where we rode out another squall. Weather moderated with clear spots in the sky. Decided worst was over and headed for Tavernier. About 5:00 a heavy rainstorm came up from the NW and we anchored for the night just below Dove Key. Rained great guns. Everybody and everything wet.

6. For a brief biography of Maxwell Smith, see Baily (1962). Smith's 1937 book contains detailed instructions for collecting mollusks as well as recommendations for specimen preservation, labeling, collection organization, catalog keeping, and much else besides. Smith's role in fostering scientific expertise among young local collectors is described by Bayer (2001), and his mollusk-dredging project in Lake Worth is mentioned in Voss (n.d.).

Chapter 1. Prohis and Fish Wardens

1. A legendary Florida lawman, Robert C. (Bob) Baker organized the hunt for the notorious Ashley gang of bank robbers and planned the ambush on Sebastian Inlet Bridge where the entire gang was shot to death in 1924. Later he personally tied the knot that hanged James Alderman, a rum runner popularly known as the "Gulf Stream pirate," who was executed at Miami for murdering two coastguardsmen and a Secret Service agent (Ling 2007).

Family lore has it that Sheriff Baker telephoned my grandparents' house one day to tell them that the Ashley gang had robbed a local bank and were last seen heading toward Hypoluxo. The purpose of the phone call was doubtless to warn everyone to stay indoors, but Grandfather was not home and Grandmother was sick and tired of hearing about the Ashleys. She carried her rocker out into the middle of Federal Highway (then a one-lane shell road), where she sat all afternoon with her shotgun, waiting for the bank robbers. Fortunately for all concerned, they must have taken another route. She was probably disappointed.

2. The rum runners came from the Bahamas, the outermost islands

of which (Grand Bahama, Gun Cay, Cat Cay, Bimini) are within sixty miles of the Florida coast. According to Foster (1991), as many as fifty or sixty speedboats loaded with liquor sometimes made the nightly run from Bimini during Prohibition. Each two-man speedboat crew was paid $1,500 per round trip: big money in the Depression and an irresistible inducement to smuggling. One contemporary newspaper account declared that "prohibition is the greatest opportunity for the Bahamas since piracy went out of style" (Buchanan 1970). Rum-running also provided a welcome source of much needed cash for many down-at-the-heels fishing communities along the southeast coast of Florida. The repeal of the 18th amendment in 1933 was not universally applauded.

3. Small craft did not need to have the drawbridge raised. The boys made their rowboat seem much larger in the dark by using a fog horn, mounting running lights, and raising a lantern on a pole, all subterfuges that were revealed to the bridge tender once they had passed through.

Chapter 2. "Power in de hold, mon!"

1. For technical accounts of the gill nets and gill-netting methods used in the south Florida mackerel and mullet fisheries during the first half of the twentieth century, see Siebenaler (1955) and Klima (1959). Gill nets are history in Florida now. The state's constitutional amendment banning the use of gill nets—approved by voters in 1994—effectively ruined hundreds of fishermen's families and devastated artisanal fishing communities on both coasts, further impoverishing an already politically and economically marginalized industry (Smith et al. 2003).

2. Fire extinguishers made by the Pyrene Manufacturing Company were filled with carbon tetrachloride, a fire retardant that may have been popularly known as "pyrene" by association

3. "Fire in the water" is bioluminescence caused by microscopic algae (dinoflagellates) that emit light in response to turbulence, such as that caused by fish activity.

Chapter 3. Cap Knight and the Bear

1. The construction and operation of big beach seines in Florida is described by Siebenaler (1955). Commercial beach seining, like gill-netting, is extinct in the state today.

2. One of the more colorful characters of Prohibition-era Florida, Eugene T. ("Cap") Knight was born at Cape Canaveral in 1871 and ran

off to sea at the age of thirteen. According to Ling (2007), he worked his way up the maritime shipping hierarchy over the next thirty years, eventually becoming a master on the Morgan Line steamers that sailed between New York and New Orleans. Retiring from legitimate seafaring just as Prohibition began, he got in on the ground floor of the far more lucrative trade in illegal booze, ferrying liquor in fast speedboats from Bimini to Hillsboro Inlet.

Soon after the 1928 hurricane, Cap bought a derelict barge, floated it up into the mangroves on a high tide, and converted it into a speakeasy and casino. The Club Unique (as it was then known) opened for business in 1929. Among its famous—or infamous—patrons over the next few decades were Franklin Roosevelt, Winston Churchill, Al Capone, Meyer Lansky, Errol Flynn, and assorted Vanderbilts and Rockefellers.

The Knight family was allied to the Vosses by marriage. Cap's brother, Thomas Knight, was keeper of the Hillsboro Lighthouse from 1911 to 1936, and Frederick Voss married his daughter, Mary Knight (Cap's niece), in 1937. Burnham and Ellis Knight, both of whom appear later in these stories, were Frederick's brothers-in-law.

Chapter 4. The Cast-Netters

1. The best early description of Lake Worth is in Pierce (1970), and much of its subsequent transformation is described in one of Gil's unpublished manuscripts (Voss n.d.), a long lament for the lagoon's sorry current state, largely the result of runaway development, bulkheading, and pollution.

Chapter 5. Snapper Fishermen

1. The early history of the Gulf snapper fishery is reasonably well documented, with good technical accounts by Jarvis (1935), Camber (1955), and Carpenter (1965). An entertaining first-hand narrative of life among Gulf snapper fishermen at sea and in port was written by Hunt (1942), and Raupp (2007) provides an interesting sociological description of the fleet based at Pensacola.

2. Not all of the Gulf snapper fleet was manned by crackers. Contemporaneous accounts of the fleet based at Pensacola describe the fisherman as including "Yankees" (New Englanders), Nova Scotians, Scandinavians, and Italians, although their debauched behavior ashore was evidently much the same as that of the cracker crews at Carrabelle (Hunt 1942).

Chapter 6. Tight Lines!

1. For period photographs of early sportfishing in Palm Beach County—but not, unfortunately, much supporting historical detail—see DeVries (2008). Apparently the first sailfish played on rod and reel in south Florida were caught on charterboats out of Miami, from which the sport spread up the coast to Fort Lauderdale, Boynton, and Stuart (Tinsley 1964). Gil's technical report on the biology of sailfish (Voss 1953) was followed by three popular articles on the same topic (Voss 1954, 1956a, 1956b), all based in part on the experiences here described in detail for the first time.

Chapter 7. The Crooked Greeks

1. See Wynne and Moorehead (2010) for an account of Florida's role in World War II. The U-boat peril gradually receded as shipping was convoyed and other sensible precautions, previously urged by the British but ignored by the U.S. Navy high command, were belatedly taken. The danger of coastal espionage was perhaps always overblown, at least in Florida waters.

2. The early history of the Florida sponge fishery up to the advent of hard-hat diving in 1905 was reviewed by Witzell (1998). Bernard (1965) described the traditional methods and equipment used by the Greek diving fleet at Tarpon Springs, and Bernard (1967) documented the appalling casualty rate of traditional Greek sponge diving in the Mediterranean.

3. According to Coast Guard records in the National Archives, Gil's crew on CG 41009 consisted of Frank H. Kenward (Coxswain, another Florida boy), Charles H. Haight (Fireman Second Class, from New York), William H. Simmons (Seaman Second Class, from Texas), Newton C. Van Voorhis (Seaman Second Class, also from Texas), and Willard H. Howard (Seaman Second Class, from Florida). The CG 41009 arrived at Tarpon Springs from Miami on January 15, 1943.

4. Gunner's mate was not his official Coast Guard rating, but Simmons' station at General Quarters was behind the .50-caliber machine gun on CG 41009 (Coast Guard records, National Archives).

Chapter 8. The Viveros

1. The best description of the live wells found in Gulf fishing schooners is in Jarvis (1935), and the best Spanish-language account seems to

be Leal's (1971). There is very little in English-language fisheries litera- ture concerning the Cuban *viveros*. Gil's account of these vessels, which were anachronisms even in the 1940s, may be the only first-hand de- scription. Soon after the war most of the Cuban fishing fleet converted to diesel power and began preserving their catch on ice (Martínez 1948; Leal 1971; Tashiro and Coleman 1977). The term *vivero* is based on *vivo* (alive), and the ice-bearing ships that eventually replaced them were known as *neveros* (from *nieve*, snow).

2. Guano racks were large wooden platforms built on pilings in shal- low offshore water to attract seabirds, whose droppings were periodi- cally harvested for fertilizer. On the Gulf Coast, guano racks were built between Tampa and Apalachee bays, where the decaying pilings are now popular spots to fish for snapper and houndfish.

3. According to Leal (1971), the *vivero* fishery was mostly based on grouper, then regarded as coarse fare and usually found on tables of the urban working class. Snapper were more highly esteemed and com- manded a higher market price in Havana.

Chapter 9. Crystal River Oystermen

1. Schlesselman (1955) described the traditional oyster fishery of the Gulf of Mexico and the many factors that may have led to its mid- twentieth-century decline. Early accounts of the Florida oyster fishery are in Ruge (1898) and Swift (1898). The use of oyster tongs is described by Siebenaler (1955).

2. Clyde R. Everett, Motor Machinist's Mate Second Class on CG 42028, hailed from Kopperl, Texas (Coast Guard records, National Ar- chives).

Chapter 10. Cedar Key

1. The turtle nets used in Florida waters are described by Siebenaler (1955) and the Florida green turtle fishery is described by Ingle and Smith (1949) and Witzell (1994). Nowadays it seems strange to talk about eating turtle, but when I was growing up in the 1960s, no trip to Key West was complete without a much-anticipated dinner of turtle steaks at one of the seafood restaurants down near the turtle pens. In fact, few gourmets of the last century ever passed up an opportunity to eat turtle. Even Archie Carr, patron saint of sea turtle conservation, relished every meal of green turtle described in his lyrical Caribbean travel diaries (Carr 1956).

2. The grisly circumstances of this lynching, in which the local justice of the peace and a constable were apparently complicit, are described by McCarthy (2007). The event itself took place in 1932.

Chapter 11. Filimingo, by God

1. Guy Bradley's story is well told by McIver (2003), one of whose primary sources was Uncle Charlie's posthumously published narrative of an 1885 plume-hunting expedition (Pierce 1962). Guy was a teenage member at the outset of that expedition, but occasional plume hunting was just how pioneer boys earned pocket money, and it was perfectly legal at the time. Guy was hired as an Audubon warden in 1902, soon after laws were passed to protect plume birds and their rookeries from industrial-scale slaughter by professional hunters. According to McIver (2003), the tombstone that Gil saw on that deserted beach in 1934 read:

GUY M. BRADLEY
1870–1905
FAITHFUL UNTO DEATH
AS GAME WARDEN OF MONROE
COUNTY HE GAVE HIS LIFE FOR
THE CAUSE TO WHICH HE WAS
PLEDGED

2. Travis McGee was a character in a wildly popular series of 1970s crime novels set in Florida. The BUSTED FLUSH was his houseboat, with which he often traversed the mangrove coast.

3. Charles Andrews' fishing camp, built in 1945, was one of three fish houses operating at Flamingo in the late 1940s, just before the park was established; altogether some fifty to seventy-five commercial fishermen were associated with these outfits. The other fish companies were run by Lloyd "Barrelhead" House and Loren Roberts (Tebeau 1963, 1968).

4. This was presumably the E. T. Knight Fish Company camp, locally managed by Ellis Knight, one of Frederick's brothers-in-law. "Boggy Bight" does not appear on any modern map of the Flamingo region that I have seen, but it might have been a contemporaneous synonym for Snake Bight, where the Knight family setup was located just northeast of Flamingo.

5. Gil is referring to the DONNYGILL, described in the foreword.

The clients who chartered the family's yacht for this particular excursion are unknown.

6. The Roberts clan originally came from Orlando. The patriarch, locally known as "Uncle Steve," settled at Flamingo in 1901. He ran a hotel out of his two-story house from 1915 to 1926, when the building was destroyed by a hurricane. His son Loren Roberts owned and operated the fish house at the time of Gil's visit. Back in Prohibition days, presumably when Gil's father and Cousin Walter stayed there, the local moonshine was known as "Cape Sable Augerdent" (a corruption of the Spanish *aguardiente*, a spirit distilled from fermented sugarcane juice). Tebeau (1968) describes the Flamingo product as "a fearsomely powerful brew that was never forgotten by the uninitiated after the first drink."

7. This name appears as Chokoloskee on modern maps, but Gil consistently spelled it Chokoluskee, possibly a local phonetic variant.

8. By all accounts the mosquitoes at Flamingo were almost insufferable. They were so numerous that, according to Tebeau (1968), an old Flamingo resident was unimpressed by the government's promise that new control measures could kill 95 percent of the pests. "You wouldn't miss 'em," he said.

Afterword

1. Smith's expansive vision for a marine laboratory at Miami was laid out in an editorial in *Science* magazine (Smith 1946) that is still worth reading as a useful summary of just how much remained unknown about many basic aspects of tropical oceanography at the middle of the last century.

2. The quoted passage is from Voss (1956: 859).

3. The quoted passage is from Voss (1971: 780).

4. Sweeney and Roper (1991) listed 21 students of cephalopods whose graduate research Gil supervised, and they estimated that some 200 publications ultimately resulted from this work. Summarizing his lifetime impact in the field, they remarked that "hardly a paper has been published in cephalopod systematics and zoogeography, and even other aspects of cephalopod biology and fisheries, that doesn't cite at least one paper published by Voss. This has been the case for nearly 4 decades, and it will continue to be so for many decades into the 21st century."

5. These articles (Voss 1967, 1971, 1973, 1974) did much to change public perceptions at a time when there was no significant domestic fishery or market for either octopus or squid.

6. Voss (1966: 44–45). *Willemoesia*, *Polycheles*, and *Eryoneicus* are so-called blind lobsters (family Polychelidae), weird-looking eyeless deep-sea crustaceans. *Notostomus* and *Plesiopenaeus* are deep-sea shrimps. *Vampyroteuthis* is the vampire squid. Scopelarchids are deep-sea fishes with telescopic eyes capable of seeing in near total darkness; they are additionally remarkable for having two retinas in each eye, one for binocular dorsal vision and the other for monocular lateral vision.

Deep-sea trawling is a highly specialized technique that requires custom-designed gear, meticulous attention to detail in every aspect of the operation, and close cooperation between the ship's crew and her scientists. Few oceanographic expeditions have trawled successfully at great depths, and this exciting work has seldom been described in the non-technical literature. The most accessible accounts are in the long out-of-print volume on the famous GALATHEA expedition (Bruun et al. 1956).

7. The quoted passage is from Voss (1988: 54–55). This crucial meeting and its outcome are described in greater detail in Voss (1960, 1988) and Griswold (1965).

8. The quoted passage is from Fichtner (1988).

Bibliography

Baily, Joshua L. Jr. 1962. "Maxwell Smith, 1888–1961." *Nautilus* 76: 33–34.

Bayer, Frederick M. 2001. "Octocoral Research—Past, Present and Future." *Atoll Research Bulletin* 494: 81–106.

Bernard, H. Russell. 1965. "Greek Sponge Boats in Florida." *Anthropological Quarterly* 38(2): 41–54.

———. 1967. "Kalymnian Sponge Diving." *Human Biology* 39(2): 103–30.

Bruun, Anton F., Svend Greve, Hakon Mielche, and Ragnar Spärck, eds. 1956. *The Galathea Deep Sea Expeditions 1950–1952*. New York: Macmillan.

Buchanan, Patricia. 1970. "Miami's Bootleg Boom." *Tequesta* 30: 13–31.

Camber, C. Isaac. 1955. *A Survey of the Red Snapper Fishery of the Gulf of Mexico, with Special Reference to the Campeche Banks*. State of Florida Board of Conservation Technical Series 12.

Carpenter, James S. 1965. *A Review of the Gulf of Mexico Red Snapper Fishery*. U.S. Department of the Interior, U.S. Fish and Wildlife Service, Bureau of Commercial Fisheries Circular 208. Washington, D.C.

Carr, Archie F. 1956. *The Windward Road: Adventures of a Naturalist on Remote Caribbean Shores*. New York: Alfred A. Knopf.

DeVries, Janet. 2008. *Sport Fishing in Palm Beach County*. Charleston, S.C.: Arcadia Publishing.

Fichtner, Margaria. 1988. "The Keeper of the Reefs." *Miami Herald*, August 12, section B, 1–2.

Foster, Charles C. 1991. *Conchtown USA: Bahamian Fisherfolk in Riviera Beach, Florida*. Boca Raton: Florida Atlantic University Press.

Greenberg, Paul. 2014. *American Catch: The Fight for Our Local Seafood*. New York: Penguin.

Griswold, Oliver. 1965. *The Florida Keys and the Coral Reef*. Miami: Graywood Press.

Harris, Margaret G. 1990. *Pioneer Daughter*. N.p.: Star Publishing Company.

Hunt, Fred. 1942. "Campeche Days." In *Thirty Years of the American Neptune*, edited by E. S. Dodge, 253–66. Cambridge, Mass.: Harvard University Press.

Ingle, Robert M., and F. G. Walton Smith. 1949. *Sea Turtles and the Turtle Industry of the West Indies, Florida and the Gulf of Mexico, with Annotated Bibliography*. Coral Gables: University of Miami Press.

Jarvis, Norman D. 1935. *Fishery for Red Snappers and Groupers in the Gulf of Mexico*. U.S. Department of Commerce, Bureau of Fisheries Investigational Report 26. Washington, D.C.

Kemp, Peter. 1976. *The Oxford Companion to Ships and the Sea*. London: Oxford University Press.

Klima, Edward F. 1959. *Aspects of the Biology and Fishery for Spanish Mackerel* Scomberomorus maculatus *(Mitchill) of Southern Florida*. State of Florida, Board of Conservation Technical Series 27.

Leal, Miguel. 1971. "En la Ruta del Vivero." *Mar y Pesca* (August): 22–29.

Ling, Sally J. 2007. *Run the Rum In: South Florida during Prohibition*. Charleston, S.C.: History Press.

Martínez, Joseph L. 1948. *The Cuban Fishing Industry*. U.S. Fish and Wildlife Service, Fishery Leaflet 308. Washington, D.C.

McCarthy, Kevin. 2007. *Cedar Key, Florida: A History*. Charleston, S.C.: History Press.

McIver, Stuart B. 2003. *Death in the Everglades: The Murder of Guy Bradley, America's First Martyr to Environmentalism*. Gainesville: University Press of Florida.

Noss, Reed F. 1996. "The Naturalists Are Dying Off." *Conservation Biology* 10(1): 1–3.

Pierce, Charles W. 1962. "The Cruise of the Bonton." *Tequesta* 22: 3–63.

———. 1970. *Pioneer Life in Southeast Florida*. Edited by D. W. Curl. Coral Gables: University of Miami Press.

Pierce, Hannibal D. 1884. "Notes on the Bluefish, Mortality of Florida Fishes, Etc." *Bulletin of the United States Fish Commission* 4: 263–66.

Raupp, Jason T. 2007. "Fish On: Pensacola's Red Snapper Fishery." *Florida Historical Quarterly* 85: 324–41.

Ruge, John G. 1898. "The Oysters and Oyster-Beds of Florida." *Bulletin of the United States Fish Commission* 17: 289–96.

Schlesselman, G. W. 1955. "The Gulf Coast Oyster Industry of the United States." *Geographical Review* 45(4): 531–41.

Siebenaler, J. B. 1955. *Commercial Fishing Gear and Fishing Methods in Florida*. State of Florida, Board of Conservation Technical Series 13.

Smith, F. G. Walton. 1946. "Functions and Development of a Tropical Marine Laboratory." *Science* 103(2681): 609–11.

Smith, Maxwell. 1937. *East Coast Marine Shells*. Ann Arbor, Mich.: Edwards Brothers.

Smith, Suzanna, Steve Jacob, Michael Jepson, and Glenn Israel. 2003. "After the Florida Net Ban: The Impacts on Commercial Fishing Families." *Society and Natural Resources* 16(1): 39–59.

Sweeney, Michael J., and Clyde F. E. Roper. 1991. "Gilbert L. Voss: A Commemoration, Bibliography, and Described Taxa." *Bulletin of Marine Science* 49(1–2): 5–19.

Swift, Franklin. 1898. "The Oyster-Grounds of the West Florida Coast: Their Extent, Condition, and Peculiarities." *Bulletin of the United States Fish Commission* 17: 285–87.

Tashiro, Joseph E., and Susan E. Coleman. 1977. "The Cuban Grouper and Snapper Fishery in the Gulf of Mexico." *Marine Fisheries Review* 39(10): 1–6.

Tebeau, Charlton W. 1963. *They Lived in the Park: The Story of Man in the Everglades National Park*. Miami: University of Miami Press.

———. 1968. *Man in the Everglades: 2000 Years of Human History in the Everglades National Park*. Coral Gables: University of Miami Press.

Tinsley, Jim B. 1964. *The Sailfish, Swashbuckler of the Open Seas*. Gainesville: University of Florida Press.

Voss, Gilbert L. 1953. "A Contribution to the Life History and Biology of the Sailfish, *Istiophorus americanus* Cuv. and Val., in Florida Waters." *Bulletin of Marine Science of the Gulf and Caribbean* 3(3): 206–40.

———. 1954. "Trailing Ocean Gamesters." *Sea Frontiers* 1(1): 11–19.

———. 1956a. "Gold Coast or Sailfish Frontier." *Sea Frontiers* 2(1): 21–30. (Authorship unattributed.)

———. 1956b. "Solving Life Secrets of the Sailfish." *National Geographic Magazine* 109(6): 859–72.

———. 1960. "First Undersea Park." *Sea Frontiers* 6(6): 87–94.

———. 1966. "The R/V Pillsbury Deep-Sea Biological Expedition to the Gulf of Guinea, 1964–65. Part 1. Narrative of the Cruises." *Studies in Tropical Oceanography* 4(1): 1–60.

———. 1967. "Squids, Jet-Powered Torpedoes of the Deep." *National Geographic Magazine* 131(3): 386–411.

———. 1968. "The Orange Grove House of Refuge No. 3." *Tequesta* 28: 3–17.

———. 1971. "Shy Monster, the Octopus." *National Geographic Magazine* 140(6): 776–99.

———. 1973a. "Investigations of the Biology and Distribution of Deep-Sea Fauna, 1964–1966." In *National Geographic Research Reports: 1966 Projects*, 271–81. Washington, D.C.: National Geographic Society.

———. 1973b. "The Squid Boats Are Coming!" *Sea Frontiers* 19(4): 194–202.

———. 1974. "Octopus on the Dining Table." *Sea Frontiers* 20(4): 236–43.

———. 1976. "Investigations of the Biology and Distribution of the Tropical Atlantic Deep-Sea Faunas, 1967–1969." In *National Geographic Research Reports: 1968 Projects*, 445–52. Washington, D.C.: National Geographic Society.

———. 1988. *Coral Reefs of Florida*. Sarasota, Fla.: Pineapple Press.

———. N.d. "The Lake and the Bay." Unpublished account of the ecological deterioration of Lake Worth from prehistoric times to the 1930s.

Witzell, W. N. 1994. "The Origin, Evolution, and Demise of the U.S. Sea Turtle Fisheries." *Marine Fisheries Review* 56: 8–23.

———1998. "The Origin of the Florida Sponge Fishery." *Marine Fisheries Review* 60(1): 27–32.

Wynne, Nick, and Richard Moorehead. 2010. *Florida in World War II*. Charleston, S.C.: History Press.

Index

Page numbers in *italics* indicate illustrations.

GILBERT VOSS (1918–1989) was born to pioneer parents in Hypoluxo, Florida, and spent much of his early life as a commercial fisherman and charterboatman. After service in the U.S. Coast Guard during World War II, he attended the University of Miami and George Washington University, where he got his PhD in 1956. A marine biologist, he worked and taught for many years at the Marine Laboratory of the University of Miami (now the Rosenstiel School of Marine and Atmospheric Science) on Virginia Key. Author of numerous scientific and popular articles on marine life, fishing, and the history of oceanography, he was also active as a conservationist and was an early proponent of the John Pennekamp Coral Reef State Park on Key Largo.

~~~~~~

ROBERT S. VOSS, the author's son, grew up in Miami but now lives with his family in Tenafly, New Jersey. He is a curator at the American Museum of Natural History in New York City, where his research is focused on the evolution and ecology of South American mammals.